Movement, Voice a

Movement, Voice and Speech

A. MUSGRAVE HORNER

Methuen & Co. Ltd

First published 1970
by Methuen & Co. Ltd
11 New Fetter Lane, London EC4
© *A. Musgrave Horner 1970*
Printed in Great Britain
by Cox & Wyman Ltd
Fakenham, Norfolk

ISBN 0 416 13700 8 Hardback
ISBN 0 416 13710 5 Paperback

Distributed in the USA
by Barnes & Noble Inc

Contents

PREFACE

ACKNOWLEDGEMENTS

THE BASIS...   page 9
Today's urgent problem   9
A new look at an old idea   11
Subjective and objective evidence   19
Theory through deduction   24
Towards vital speech   31

...DYNAMIC SPEECH   43
Kinesthetic improvisation   43
Alerting the senses   52
Vocal breakthrough   56
Verbal follow-up   57
Creative interpretation   60
Significant everyday speech   95
Problems and principles   109
Technique re-assessed   115
Speech education for today   121

GLOSSARY   129
SHORT READING LIST   137
INDEX   139

Preface

In the first part of this book, I have attempted to set down ideas which I have been thinking about for a long time in regard to movement as the basis of effective speech. In the second part, I have described methods which I have found useful in carrying through these ideas into effective practice.

It should not be assumed that the theory and practice discussed and described constitute a complete course in speech. But providing the more mechanical and technical aspects of speech have been dealt with or are being concurrently studied, it may be assumed that expressional and communicational effectiveness of speech will be noticeably improved by applying the principles I have outlined to practical exercises such as I have suggested.

I do not recognize a clear-cut borderline between 'professional' standards of speech skills and the speech aptitudes required by the 'ordinary' man or woman anxious to communicate effectively with other 'ordinary' men and women in daily life. No doubt actors, broadcasters, teachers, public speakers, and others with specialized speech-needs, will be concerned with the application of their skills to clearly defined situations. But domestic and social situations make demands upon all of us if our day-to-day talk is to reflect those qualities which are anticipated from the continual development of education for living.

Whatever kind of attainment may be aimed at, I believe that the method by which it may most certainly be reached is that which I have tried to describe in this book. It is up to the reader to decide how far he is prepared to follow it in the pursuit of dynamic speech, or to what particular ends he will apply the skills he will undoubtedly acquire.

A. Musgrave Horner, 1969

Acknowledgements

Acknowledgement is due to the following for permission to use copyright material:

Mrs Hodgson and Macmillan & Co. Ltd for 'The Bells of Heaven' from *Collected Poems*; The Society of Authors as the literary representative of the estate of Laurence Binyon, for an extract from *The Builders*; Michael Joseph and David Higham Associates Ltd. for an extract from *The Chrysalids* by John Wyndham; Mr Raglan Squire and Macmillan & Co. Ltd for 'The Discovery' from *Collected Poems* (There was an Indian) by J. C. Squire; A. D. Peters & Co. for 'Driving Sheep' by Rose Macaulay; Mr Michael Ayrton for 'Fallen Cities' by Gerald Gould; Methuen & Co. Ltd for 'Happiness' by A. A. Milne; Faber & Faber for an extract from *Murder in the Cathedral* by T. S. Eliot; The Society of Authors as agent for the Bernard Shaw Estate, for an extract from *Saint Joan*; the Trustees of the Hardy Estate and Macmillan & Co. Ltd for an extract from *Tess of the D'Urbervilles*; Eric Williams and Collins Publishers for an extract from *The Wooden Horse*. The owners of the copyright of the extract from 'Coal' by John Gould Fletcher have not yet been traced, but the necessary arrangements will be made at the first opportunity.

The Basis...

Today's urgent problem

SUDDENLY THE WORLD SEEMS TO HAVE BECOME noisy with the shouting of angry mobs, and with the equally degrading spectacle of masses of suppressed pawns. Even those who neither yell nor cringe are often induced, in one way or another, to accept ideas without considering their validity, and to behave without reference to the rationality of their acts. Coercion is practised by the few to the subjugation of the many. None of this need be, of course, if all men could be prevailed upon never to exploit other men; but to entertain such a notion seems to imply escape to completely detached fantasy.

Education should offer some hope, but hysterical crowds are unlikely to heed sensible advice if it is offered by intellectual bores; and apathetic masses are not likely to be liberated by programmed instruction which dispenses information without the stimulus of relevant meaning. Objective study of coercive methods, especially in terms of mass psychology, is a possible antidote to the unscrupulous manipulation of human behaviour by biased communicational pressures. This kind of study is increasing, and more and more of us are being forewarned – and therefore forearmed; yet the study of propaganda methods is so complex that only a few will build up a personal defence against coercive tactics used against them. Meanwhile, devices openly described in current literature on coercive communication may be perfected by those in whom selfish ambition dominates social conscience.

Human communication having deteriorated largely into a system of superiority through technical impressiveness by which the many are exploited by the few, it is imperative that the declared ideal of freedom of speech shall be made real by offering to all the chance to overcome the monopoly of the few. Fortunately there is an alternative to the use of coercive stunts to trap the unwary. Legitimately persuasive skills may be developed through methods which aim at expressing thought and feeling as directly as possible in voice and speech. Working towards consistency between belief and its expression, we shall discover that sincerity rather than a compromise of manipulated ideas and calculated appeal to emotion, is more gratifying to a speaker, more beneficial to his listeners and, in the long run, more effective as communication. If it be thus based, speech education is the solution to the problem providing that we clear away, with one final sweep, the last remnants of methods which were little better than means of applying stereotyped 'expression' to speech, with negligible concern for the uniqueness of each speaker.

Normally, our speech is acquired largely by unconscious imitation of the speech patterns already established in the environments to which we are exposed. The noise level and the aesthetic qualities of the sounds we hear daily; the physical atmosphere – be it cold, dry, warm, humid, clean or vitiated; the professions of our parents, friends, ourselves; the kind of education we received, and the level to which we pursued it; our social life; every aspect, in fact, of our entire cultural environment is likely to affect our speech habits quite automatically. Acquired in this natural way, speech becomes integrated with the concurrently maturing personality, ultimately settling into an eclectic pattern which is individualistic and which significantly reveals the character of the speaker.

On the other hand, undue pressure consciously to improve speech as a detached physical skill, may open an irreparable rift between a speaker and his speech. The only part of speech which might necessitate deliberate imitation is that part which concerns the formation of the most widely acceptable phonemes as the basis of maximum intelligibility. Narrowly conceived speech training does little more than this.

All other aspects of oral expression are best developed by creatively intensifying a speaker's sense of individual involvement in and identification with thoughts and feelings which he considers worthy of communicating to others. Enlightened methods of speech training always have such a principle well in mind.

How this integration of thought, feeling, expression and communication may be achieved, is the purpose of this book.

A new look at an old idea

Hunches are usually exciting and are frequently profitable. They result from creative perception. Many scientific discoveries, technological inventions, educational developments, social reforms, religious revivals, and works of literature and art, have resulted from imaginative hunches or, if you prefer the phrase, from inspired guesses. Speech communication is no exception to this generalization. Whether it be in the investigation of its nature, the devising of methods to improve personal aptitude in speaking, or the application of such aptitudes to theatre, platform, pulpit or lectern, specialists in speech communication have depended a great deal upon hunches.

Mere gimmicks and unworthy stunts have, to the shame of their perpetrators, fooled some of the people some of the time, but much of the best training in oral communication has been developed through long processes of trial and error having proved the validity of an initial hunch. Most significant among hunches in speech communication during recent years have been those concerned with the inseparable relationships between bodily movement, voice and speech communication. From earliest times there have been acknowledgements of such an integration. Ancient Greek culture, wholesome in its regard for physical poise and mastery of the spoken word among the bases of its educational system, recognized the human importance of both movement and speech. Investigators into the origins of language have recognized the gestural basis of speech. Speech therapists have found that to release expression through movement sometimes releases expression through speech.

The combined significance of such evidence has not always been properly interpreted. The action of 'speaking verse with gesture' has at times produced quite grotesque results. 'Deportment classes' have often resulted in statuesque inflexibility of bodily expression thwarting the attempts of the mind to break through personality barriers into communicative speech.

Nevertheless, a true realization of the essence of movement–voice–speech relationships has been growing rapidly
during the past twenty-five years or so. In fact, I remember
(when I was a student) one of my teachers, helping me to
increase my range of tonal variety, saying, 'Get the right
facial expression and you can't help getting the right tone.
Let the face show what you are feeling, and the tone will
follow automatically.' Unfortunately, he then proceeded
to explain the timing (the technical co-ordination) of
gesture, facial expression, voice and speech. He took me
so close to enlightenment, and then confused me by his
reference to timing. But they were very technical days,
and he could hardly be blamed for teaching consistently
with what was then the generally accepted method –
through discipline to learn the techniques of vocal expression so well (albeit somewhat mechanically) that they
would never falter under stress of public utterance!

But the seed took root and, although I soon learnt to
mistrust the idea of meticulously organizing the timing of
movement with speech, I realized that the face and the
voice are indeed varied by the action of the same, or of
closely associated, muscles. Yet, not one of my teachers
(and, in their day, they were very good teachers) had
mentioned that it is the relationship (between movement,
voice and speech) that is of real expressional significance.

Some methods which were used to improve articulatory
firmness had the unfortunate result of causing over-tensing
of associated muscles and consequent harshness of tone.
I discovered for myself that the degree of articulatory
firmness is a concentration of the general tonus of a
speaker's entire muscular system; that, in this general
way, the relationship between muscular tonicity and firmness of speech is entirely natural, whereas the isolation of

articulatory control from bodily tonicity is artificial and leads to over-concern with elocution.

A phenomenon which fascinated me when its significance dawned upon me was the way in which members of an audience tend involuntarily to mimic a good performer on stage, and I sensed that it is this kind of audience response which consolidates the process of 'getting it across'. The performer's contact with his audience is ensured when they feel the emotions which are expressed by his movement by the impulse to make similar movements themselves. I noticed that good orchestral conductors have much more to do than merely to 'beat time'. Realizing the irresistibility of emotionally expressive movement, I no longer tried to defeat nature by keeping out-of-step with a Salvation Army band if I were caught in the street when they were parading (although to this day I still feel rather foolish in such circumstances). I understood why I had gone home healthily tired (but by no means irritably fatigued) after attending evocative performances of uninhibited dancing – especially African, Caribbean, Spanish and Chinese – because my muscles had been alerted in sympathy with those of the performers. I became convinced that human communication is basically kinesthetic, that is to say, it is dependent upon sensations of muscular response to thought and feeling in both transmission and reception. I began to find meaning in much that I had witnessed too early in life to understand; why, for instance, many men who would not have volunteered on their own volition to join the fighting forces in the First World War, would find a military band quite irresistible and, once having found themselves marching in step to the beat, were ready to speak a loyal oath with similar compulsive conformity.

Looking back, it seems only natural that voice, and more especially the highly evolved skills of speech, would have been noticed as extensions of the more basic communication through movement. People who looked tired, spoke lethargically. A sick child moaned; an excited child stuttered. A drunken man would slur his foolish rationalizations, while his angry wife spat her staccato vituperation at him. The awareness that the deep-seated relationship between movement, voice and speech is more important than their segregated effectiveness, alerted me to the futility of attempting to develop dynamic speech other than from expressive movement.

Once convinced that the combined effects of movement, voice and speech are infinitely greater than the sum of their separate effectiveness, PROVIDING ONLY THAT THE RELATIONSHIPS BETWEEN THEM ARE UNDERSTOOD AND APPLIED, I began consistently to emphasize my conviction in my teaching. But teaching was too frequently prescribed by the requirements of (not highly imaginative) examinations. Also, the exploration of movement–voice–speech relationships was almost always restricted by the physical limitation of class-rooms which sometimes had a platform for me, but only desks screwed to the floor for my students. During the last twenty or so years, however, I have become increasingly aware of a new spirit of inquiry into the nature of effective speaking. I believe that this is happening only just in time before the more humane aspects of human speech are crushed by the impact of modern (mainly electronic) communication technology.

It is, of course, sensible that we avail ourselves of every improved technological aid to the investigation of communication. But in practical communicational situations it is urgent that the identity of the individual speaker shall not be swamped by modern communication technology in operation. The individual must remain responsible for his speaking, in spite of interference by transmission and distribution technologists who have the power to modify a speaker's message, or by TV presentation officers who may attempt to control a speaker's 'public image'. Modern communication technology is infinitely more insidious in modifying a speaker's intentions than ever the Press has been in using clever journalistic skill to distort a speaker's words.

In view of such menaces (not to mention the general sociological problems arising from them), who can afford not to guard by every means at his disposal the rights of individual speech? Styles of speech which may well be suitable when speaking through a modern electronic communication system, may be entirely unsuitable when speaking unaided by such devices. Yet the methods demanded by the former kind of situation permeate (often to the disadvantage of) the latter which depend entirely upon the speaker's unaided skill. An actor may spend so much of his time in a radio or TV studio as to find himself at a disadvantage on stage; a clergyman or politician may adapt his style to broadcasting or television to such an extent as to become comparatively ineffective in the pulpit or on the platform. The young woman who announces train departures and arrivals at a main-line station may go through life disappointingly single if she addresses her boyfriends in her railway-platform manner! The preservation of vital, technologically-unaided speech demands the urgent attention of speech practitioners. An effective stimulus to such preservation could result from a clearer understanding and a more intense application of the kinesthetic basis of effective speech. But, although professional opinion generally is no longer in doubt about the inter-action of movement, voice and speech, the understanding of such interaction is largely intuitive and, in application, depends too much upon hunches.

Now too much teaching by trial and error can be waste-ful of effort and may be disastrous in its results. However pleasantly euphemistic it may be to describe such teaching as empirical, it is less pleasant to note that a variant of the same word may denote a quack. I feel sure that the number of quacks among teachers of speech is no greater than in any other profession, but if we wish to avoid any imputation of quackery, then we must move beyond the stage of empirical teaching to scientifically-based methods. System-atic method is one of the hall-marks of professionalism. An area which is waiting to be systematically explored to the benefit of speech training is that of the relationship between movement, voice and speech. We know a great deal about each of the three related parts, but are by no means clear about how each serves the others to make the overall effect of the three parts, rightly integrated, im-measurably greater than the mere sum of them if developed separately – which still happens too frequently.

For instance, on the staffs of reputable speech-training institutions will be found specialists in speech and special-ists in movement, each acknowledging the status of the other, but often leaving their students bewildered as to how the one communicational medium is complementary to the other. I have had adequate opportunity to observe the results of such confusion in students who, after such training, have become teachers.

Many make creditable attempts at teaching the oral patterns of spoken English, but with a superficiality which disregards the real basis of effective communication. Their pupils acquire a manner of speaking which is no more than a veneer which momentarily appears attractive, but which offends when (as inevitably happens) it wears so thin that it ceases to conceal the inferior craftsmanship which it was intended to disguise. Others have based their teaching on mime, creative movement, improvisation and dance–drama with spectacularly dramatic results. But I have found that many such teachers do not produce more effective speakers from their pupils, in spite of the liberation of their expression through movement. The transfer of expressive skill from movement to speech has frequently been either negligible or (at best) not commensurate with the time and effort involved, even though 'it's all tremendous fun!' Only occasionally do perceptive teachers successfully relate movement and speech to the improvement of their pupils' oral communication, and it is the methods of these teachers which should be systematized. It is they who have proved the effectiveness of the kinesthetically based transfer of a speaker's mind to his voice and speech, and a similarly based transfer to the mind of the listener.

Communication thus conceived develops through a more widely extended sequence than is customarily recognized. The receptor senses are intensely involved. Sensory imagery is vital. Muscular tonus is not only visibly but also vocally expressed. The kinesthetic sense is the common indispensable factor throughout the entire communicational process.

Speaker and listener become mutually involved to an extent which cannot be realized as a result of the mere study of the rationale of effective speaking. Speakers who are well-informed about orthodox speech theory are not necessarily effective in their own oral communications.

Abstruse communication theory may, in fact, lure a student away from speech as real experience. A kinesthetic approach to speech communication ensures a depth of involvement which integrates speech communication into a total experience shared by speaker and listener.

This book is based on notes which I have collated over many years during which I have observed, read about, thought on, and experimented with, the relation between movement, voice and speech. I hope that the following sections will lead to discussion and argument through which enlightenment may come, stimulating the kind of experimentation through which more effective speech communication may be achieved.

Subjective and objective evidence

Information about movement–voice–speech relationships may be ascertained from many sources. Most immediately, day-to-day observations will verify that a relationship does indeed exist. Gesticulation, change of posture, facial expression, are immediately apparent when we watch people speaking. Bodily action of great variety is part and parcel of speech situations.

That such movement is no merely superficial accompaniment to speech may be deduced from the frequency with which a speaker's gestural mannerisms coincide with such hesitations as may interrupt his fluency. It really does seem as if the finger-thumb-snap, or the head-scratch, or the tapping of a finger on the table, helps a speaker to resume his talk before a pause becomes embarrassingly prolonged; that such actions are not merely devices for 'filling the pause', but are, in some very definite way, responsible (if only partly) for resumption of fluency.

It is obvious that gesture reinforces the emphatic word. It is also patently clear that 'emphatic gestures' are not just visual indications of stressed words. Their use is such a natural kind of behaviour that to suppress them, by discipline only, will almost certainly rob speech of emphatic vocal intensity. Movement substitutes for speech when the spoken word would be inadequate for the occasion. When feelings are too deep for words, the hand-clasp and similar kinds of gestures take over as a matter of course.

Appropriate mood or atmosphere is established by movement in advance of, and carried over into, the speech that follows it. This is apparent at a cocktail party sponsored by a nervous hostess, or at the annual meeting of the unsuccessful company in which we have sunk our hard-earned savings. However ingratiating our hostess, or mealy-mouthed the Chairman of the Board, their postural tensions (by themselves as well as by their effects upon voice and speech) communicate basic feelings with a devastating truthfulness which no subsequent words can cancel.

We may learn much from watching television. Producers imagine that they have solved the problem which arises from the fact that many good speakers and singers cannot act, and that many good actors cannot sing. Through techniques (such as 'dubbing' and 'lip-synchronizing') it is thought possible to marry the art of an actor to the art of a singer. Occasionally the stunt works. More frequently it does not; not because of the obvious technical problems involved, but because of the tell-tale incongruity between the quality of a voice recorded at comfortably low intensity close to a microphone and the visual impression of a performer exhibiting emotional intensity.

Everyday life is full of equally convincing evidence; an indulgent father unsuccessfully pretending to be stern; a tense patient 'acting tough' with quavering voice in the dentist's waiting-room, a bricklayer unable to warn his mate down below until after he has dropped the bricks, the muscular strain of carrying which had stopped him from shouting – until it was too late!

Now let us jump from the familiar present back to the very remote past. Let us speculate that man has derived a gesture–voice–speech relationship from pre-human antiquity; that speech in the evolution of man had its origins in movement. Among the many hypotheses about the origins of speech in the human race, two of the most plausible have relevance to our present topic.

The GESTURE THEORY was formulated by Wilhelm Wundt, a nineteenth-century psychologist.[1] Wundt argued that as there is a consistent relationship between sensory reception and its consequent expression, gesture not only expresses an individual's feelings and ideas, but will evoke similar feelings and ideas in the minds of others.

Sir Richard Paget's name is associated with the ORAL GESTURE THEORY.[1] It may be argued that Paget developed Wundt's theory, in that Paget postulated that as man became increasingly involved occupationally, his limbs became less and less available for gesture language. Tongue and lips therefore took over the making of gesture with the added advantage that when vocalized they became

---

[1] For further reading reference should be made to *Elements of Folk Psychology* by Wilhelm Wundt (trans. Schaub), New York, Macmillan and *Human Speech* by Sir Richard Paget, London, Routledge.

'audible gestures' and therefore infinitely more resourceful communicationally.

I see much more than purist significance in these theories. I see evidence of an association between movement, voice and speech, of such close affinity as to be indissoluble – except at the risk of injury to the conjoined parts. Injury has already been done. Speech has become divorced from experience as language has become more consciously abstract and symbolic. Words are no longer labels attached to experiences; they are for most of us, and for most of the time, labels which have never been attached to experience. In this respect most speech today is as spurious as the stickers on a con-man's suitcase.

Although modern educational psychologists appear to see little practical significance in the recapitulation theory of human development, I believe that there is much significance in the fact that, during our first years of life, we do apparently recapitulate an order of language development consistent with the theories of Wundt and Paget, the significance being in the genetic plausibility of that which modern speech educationists have empirically discovered, that expressive speech develops best from expressive movement. On the other hand, consistent application of this thesis has been more tenuous, as is implied by the way in which teachers of voice and speech have sometimes sought to find in the arts of mime, traditional ballet, and modern dance, 'aids' to voice and speech training. The results have too often been little more than that achieved by an artificial grafting of several incompatible sets of skills.

Yet we may learn much from the great imaginative leaders in the field of expressive movement. Rudolf Laban's concept of expressive movement, with its virtually unlimited expressional permutations, has been a source of inspiration to many imaginative teachers of voice and speech. Emile Jacques-Dalcroze's 'Eurhythmics', an education in the arts with its emphasis on rhythm and gymnastics evoking mind, ear and body into simultaneous involvement in music, is a challenge to speech educationists to achieve like results in their field of responsibility. The value to speech training of such parallel systems in other arts is, however, generally indirect, depending upon a teacher's skill in adaptation, and upon the transfer of understanding and attitude from one field to the other.

Common factors in the fields of movement and speech are those concepts of creative expression and dynamic communication which are common to both. To compare the worst of one with the best of the other is not necessarily unfair if the terms of comparison are clearly admitted, and it might be salutory for all concerned with the teaching of speech to recognize that the gulf between a rehearsal of a Covent Garden Ballet and a routine 'deportment class' at a third-rate school of speech and drama, is as wide as musicians would recognize between a 'Music through Movement' class (conducted imaginatively on 'Dalcroze' lines) and 'Action Songs' organized by a dispirited infant-teacher in an overcrowded class-room.

What is important to teachers of voice and speech is that any kind of creative experience is good for them and their pupils. When such creative experience, however, involves movement, then their aim should be to discover from it any way in which it may be genuinely integrated into their work towards improvement of oral communication. For there is no doubt at all that effective communication is movement-based.

Theory through deduction

This is not a chapter of theory (much theory has already been incidentally stated), but a few words about modifications to current speech-training theory which, in general lags behind the noticeable advances which have been taking place in the practice of modern speech education.

During the last decade or two, the most progressive teachers of speech have reorientated themselves within the infinitely wider field of communication, enriching their own specific knowledge and understanding of speech processes by a realization that the only ultimate justification of their work is its contribution to the wide range of integrated skills and knowledge which enable people to communicate effectively. But in their exciting exploration of hitherto ignored subjects, such as semantics, psycholinguistics, acoustic-phonetics and (to the more adventurous) into cybernetics and information theory, they have allowed the lure of the new to detract from their own particular responsibilities to voice and speech theory which is significant in its own right as a legitimate part of communication theory.

I suppose that the bulk of conventional theory based largely on a mechanistic view of unmotivated voice and speech is useful. Information in areas such as physiology, phonology and phonetics is given as a matter of course in almost all books on speech training. An intelligent student, training under the guidance of a conscientious teacher, is almost certain to develop qualities of voice and speech restricted only to the limits obtainable from the particular vocal and articulatory organs with which he (the student) has been endowed.

Expressional devices, generalizations of observed characteristics of effective speakers in action, are also described in most books on speech training. These, too, are useful in that they establish certain vocal conventions which at least enable an unmotivated speaker to convey ideas with a reasonable hope of their being understood. But such descriptions of expressive modulation, when recommended as models, tend to restrict rather than encourage individuality in speaking.

Examples of the need to speak efficiently in unmotivated situations may be cited in considerable numbers. Radio news-reading is a good example of a profession dependent upon a clear scheme of conventional expression which enables information to be disseminated without revealing the reader's personal reactions to it. Knowing the 'rules' of modulation, and applying them with mechanical skill, might be useful to a third-rate repertory actor when called upon to play part after part in a season of theatrical pot-boilers; to a preacher foolish enough to repeat verbatim a sermon which satisfied a congregation and gratified his homiletic ambitions on a previous occasion; to a school teacher compelled to give a lesson in which he is not interested; or to a policeman lugubriously reading in a magistrate's court his report of a minor traffic offence. But these are not examples of dynamic speech, and few of us would care to suffer continual subjection to occupational restrictions which forbid personal involvement in statements we are required to utter. On such occasions as we might be called upon to communicate information only, we need to rely upon linguistic, semantic, vocal and phonemic theories which are already well-stated in many reputable books. Traditional modulation theory will be useful to us in those situations in which our speech needs efficiently to inform about matters in which we may not be deeply involved.

But there is urgent need to re-state the theory of modulation so that expression is not merely described as a model for imitation, but is explained as the result of the sincere release of individual thought and feeling. Only by the application of such a re-statement of theory shall we be able finally to eliminate the hypocrisy of speech which contrives to sound sincere but which is nothing more than the imitation of described symptoms of sincerity. Instead of catering for mere poseurs, we shall be more able to help the statesman with a sense of commitment, the dedicated preacher, the teacher with a true sense of vocation, and the actor who really wants to penetrate into his roles. It should not be our responsibility to cater for anyone who is content only to simulate the external symptoms of sincerity. It is our duty to help all who desire that their speech shall consistently reveal their own convictions. If any of our students subsequently use their acquired skills for purposes of deception, our conscience should be clear in that we have played no conscious part in training speakers for unworthy purposes.

To be adequate, theory of speech expression should begin by considering individual linguistic development and end with semantic control of words in communication. From birth (if not before) sensations and perceptions are stored, to be recalled by one or other of the processes of memory without their original causal stimuli. The substitution of words for actual experiences is of undeniable convenience, but it holds equally the terrible consequences of symbols taking the place of real experience. Skill in the manipulation of symbols may well be the basis of abstract thinking, but imagination is stimulated most intensively by creative reconfigurations of sensations recollected as experience – not merely identified by the symbols that have classified them in our memories.

Verbally codified experience is restrictive, and requires the most conscientious discipline if it is not to distort a description or analysis of experience even when a speaker intends to be sincere. Semantics attempts to help us to say what we mean. To consider the sequence of linguistic processes from their experiential beginnings to semantically controlled utterance is essential to a speaker who wishes to *talk* sense. But to *communicate* sense *evocatively*, a speaker needs to understand the process of paralinguistic reinforcement which helps a sincere speaker to show that he *means* what he says.

It is in this respect that the kinesthetic sense is vital to an understanding of the means by which real experience, is expressed whether concurrently or retrospectively in vigorous speech, and by which vicarious experience may most nearly approximate to real experience. Kinesthetic theory is therefore basic to the intelligent acquirement of effective speech, whether creative or interpretational. It is relevant to the whole process of paralinguistic reinforcement of the spoken word, from sensory perception (without which no experience is possible) to the ultimate communication of such experience to others through the medium of spoken language. It is especially relevant to kinesic movement which accompanies speech as gesture, facial expression, stance and posture. It is supremely relevant when understood as the explanation of voice and speech vitalized by the oral effects of muscular tonicity.

Knowledge of the sense organs, and of their connection through the nervous system to the body's reacting mechanisms, is essential. Moreover, it is extremely important

that we break, once and for all, from the popular but restrictive notion of there being but five senses – sight, hearing, smell, taste, and touch – and include other senses recognized in modern psychology, such as the sense of pain, of temperature and, most vitally for the student of speech, the sense of kinesthesis. To study the sense organs is to become aware of them as the starting-point of all personal experience; once aware of their nature and the processes through which they function, the systematic development of their acuity through increasing ranges of perception, and their conservation, become matters of great concern.

As dynamic speech cannot be other than the expression of zestful experience, the only means by which such experience can be personally initiated, or vicariously shared, should be understood. The starting-point of theory specific to our topic must be the adequate consideration of the senses. Information is readily available on the sense organs, the central nervous system, and the organization of connections between sensory stimulus and its resultant bodily responses. Special attention should be paid to the autonomic nervous system which is concerned with emotionally stimulated bodily changes among which, and all-important to an understanding of paralinguistic effects, is the relationship between muscular tonus and emotion. The fact that muscles are both motor mechanisms and sense organs is the crux of the general kinesthetic link between emotional experience and its expression kinesically, whilst the particular response of the muscles associated with the vocal organs is solely responsible for the registration of emotion through voice and speech. Not only is there muscular response to emotion, but a response is known to be made.

This neuro-muscular basis of human expression has been accepted as a matter of course by speech therapists, but too rarely by teachers of practical speech. A number of modern specialists have, however, developed systems which apply the theory empirically. If theory is considered desirable, then it should be extended, beyond the merely descriptive information about muscles and their movements during voice production and speech formation, to the cause of such movements and the reasons why they are naturally indicative of a speaker's feelings.

Theory developed from this fundamental base has many advantages in practical applications; it is enlightening to students who conceive vocal inflection, for instance, to be only a matter of 'raising the voice to indicate an incomplete statement' or 'allowing the voice to fall to indicate conclusion' (the cause, incidentally, of much inaudibility at sentence-ends and of artificial tricks to suspend pitch on an unnaturally high level which destroys the normal consolidation of a completed statement). A common method recommended to overcome the problem of inaudibility at falling inflections is the application of the 'abdominal press' whereby deliberate breath pressure is retained to the end of a phrase (when breath may be conveniently replenished) to ensure audibility on a naturally low pitch – and this method does indeed work. But once a speaker has grasped the basis idea that if mental and emotional intensity are sustained by concentration on meaningful communication, then both vocal pitch and audibility will be natural and adequate respectively as the result of the muscular tonus of all the muscles concerned with voice and speech being appropriate to the situation.

Not only is it possible and most reasonable to explain the expressional use of inflection in this way, it may also be shown that stress results from increased tonus adding intensity to those verbal units which are felt by a speaker to be relatively more significant than others. Once variations of pitch and stress are understood as inevitable physical outcomes of different intensities of thought and feeling, the entire phenomena of pitch-range, inflection, intonation, stress, emphasis and climax becomes more realistic than mere symptoms of expressive speech described (but not explained) as patterns to be imitated by speakers who are content merely with appearing to be expressive without being really involved in communicational experience.

The kinesthetic sense of rhythm transferred to voice and speech not only makes prosody redundant, but positively enables a primitive experience to be vocally applied to the more flexibly rhythmic stress of fluent prose and the more definitely patterned beat of poetry.

In the adjustment of speech-sounds to values considered socially appropriate to our environment, the aural recognition of what is desired is assisted by kinesthetic feed-back; whilst the degree of intensity with which consonants are uttered need no longer be organized by consciously applying suitable degrees of firmness to their formation (a dangerous concept in any case, because consciously applied firmness for certain utterances implies slackness – always undesirable – for others), it rather becomes a matter of lingual tonus induced (if only we encourage it) by the involvement of a speaker in a communicational situation.

Tone colour is discovered to be modifications of voice arising from resonators being changed in shape, size and degree of rigidity, as the result of emotionally stimulated muscular tonicity.

If an adequate theory of speech expression needs to acknowledge the importance of zestful sensory experience as its starting-point, it follows that the kinesthetic sense needs particular consideration because it is only through kinesthesis that any sensation can be fully experienced, expressed or communicated. Moreover, as one after another aspect of modulation is found to be fully explicable only by reference to emotionally stimulated muscular tonus, it becomes apparent that the kinesthetic sense of tonicity is indispensable to a comprehensive explanation of dynamic speech.

Towards vital speech

From among its many shades of meaning, ranging from the scientifically precise to the colloquially vague, I use the term 'Dynamic' to describe the right kind of force applied to speech in the right way – having regard to the situation in question.

Ignoring (for the time being) the casual day-to-day chattering and nattering of domestic gossip and social small-talk, speech may theoretically be classified into two extreme categories; one aiming at conveying information believed to be authentic, the other provocatively presenting a point of view, or persuading a listener to change his mind, or to coerce him into believing that which cannot be proved. The former class assumes that clear statement of logically constructed argument will generally be readily accepted by sensible listeners – it is cerebral, intellectual, scientific. In the latter class, a speaker assumes the right to reinforce his statement by revealing non-intellectual aspects of his personality, such as sincerity, enthusiasm and conviction. These two categories are hypothetical only. In reality, they are complementary; either kind may dominate, alternately, depending upon the fluctuating moods of a situation.

For example, a lecturer might begin a lecture assuming that his students are sufficiently prepared, anxious to benefit from what they hear, and intelligent enough to do so. His speech would be typical of the first category. But if, as he proceeds, he finds his suppositions to be ill-founded, he will modify his style towards that of the second category. Noticing poor response to the mere delivery of well-attested information, he attempts to evoke better response by strengthening his emphasis, by displaying personal conviction, or by other non-intellectual means.

Random comment on the news over a somewhat late and leisurely breakfast is a far cry from sonorously declaimed dialogue of stylized Greek tragedy. But both extremes may form parts of an actor's daily experience; yet he does not declaim at breakfast, nor natter his lines from the stage during classic Greek drama. A politician might grunt an odd meaningless pleasantry to his wife between bites of buttered toast, and ten minutes later browbeat his constituency into his party line. An evangelical revivalist might quite casually inquire about his children's mumps before leaving for the stadium hoping to convert thousands of gullible enthusiasts into what he would describe as a change-of-heart.

It should not be assumed, however, that our second category of speech is exclusively associated with public occasions. Although we all pass many hours commenting not very significantly about the weather, the state of the world, the generation older than ourselves, or the generation younger than ourselves, it is equally certain that at some time during almost every day we express ourselves energetically in denunciation, raillery, passionate affection (if we are young), or compassion (if we have grown old profitably).

Life would be happier if more of us could speak less defensively about the things that are nearest to our hearts. Too few of those with ideas of value have the skill to state them; too many others are impressively bombastic about trivialities. It is not by the tricks, used by slick, self-seeking charlatans to influence others to become their friends, that truth will prevail in a world of false values, but by honest convictions fearlessly expressed by speakers of integrity. Yet, sincerity by itself is not enough. To be effective communally, to make helpful impact upon our environment, we need dynamically to express what we sincerely believe. Sincerity has enormous potential energy; to be effective it needs to be released through dynamic communication.

Now although speech of our first category may differ in content from lucid intellectual argument to inconsequential social blather, its common characteristic is its lack of emotional colouring. Whether heavy or light in its informational content, it follows a sequence something like:

Through his SENSE ORGANS a speaker recognizes a situation in which he should participate.
His RECEPTION CENTRES (in the nervous system) respond and set in motion his
REASONING FACULTIES, either in a casual review of a point at issue (if the matter is familiar to the speaker), or a responsible consideration of the matter (if it is complex or, perhaps, unfamiliar to him). As he reasons,

c

or even if he merely recalls past reactions to the same topic, his

MENTAL SPEECH ORGANIZATION will formulate words which, as a result of

LINGUISTIC MOTOR ACTIVITY, he will speak to his listeners.

If his thinking has been clear, his words will be grouped and stressed sensibly, and linked by simple inflections; little else being necessary for the communication of information only.

But this is oral communication in its most restricted form, conveying little (if any) more than that which a written statement of the same message would convey. Such speech might well be called LINGUISTIC, sensibly communicating words without reinforcement by situational stimuli or as a result of emotional urges. On the other hand, dynamic speech does depend upon situational stimuli, and it expresses the intensity of a speaker's attitude to a topic under discussion, not unreasonably coercing, but attempting reasonably to persuade rather than merely to inform. Dynamic speech is, in fact, linguistically valid, but is reinforced by what might be called PARALINGUIS-TIC effects, happening alongside, indeed extending beyond the purely semantic communication of words.

If language had only a linguistic purpose, a strong case could be argued for the superiority of writing over speaking on the grounds of informational exactness and communication of meaning. Measured in terms of informational precision, a modern computer is infinitely superior to human speech. But human speech cannot be so restricted. It should involve the whole personality of man. Its physical basis is obvious, but that it involves more than

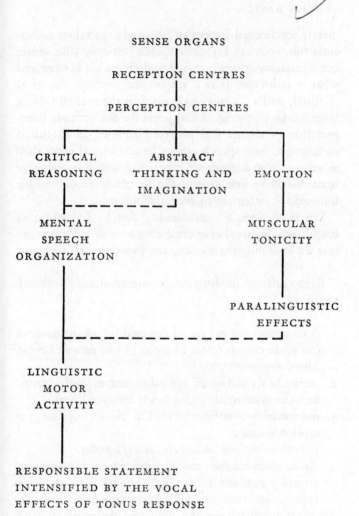

SENSE ORGANS

RECEPTION CENTRES

PERCEPTION CENTRES

CRITICAL
REASONING

ABSTRACT
THINKING AND
IMAGINATION

EMOTION

MENTAL
SPEECH
ORGANIZATION

MUSCULAR
TONICITY

PARALINGUISTIC
EFFECTS

LINGUISTIC
MOTOR
ACTIVITY

RESPONSIBLE STATEMENT
INTENSIFIED BY THE VOCAL
EFFECTS OF TONUS RESPONSE

merely intellectual processes is not always taken sufficiently into account. Dynamic speech not only talks sense, but it interests others in trying to decide what is sense and what is nonsense. It is a wholesome, perhaps the most civilized, outlet for our emotions. It is the natural vehicle intended by playwrights and poets for the ultimate interpretation of drama and poetry. Extended to its fullest conception, such speech cannot be considered other than as arising from kinesthetic experience which is operative immediately speech crosses the threshold from sensible informative statement to evocative utterance.

We have already considered a sketchy indication of linguistic sequence. Let us review the same sequence in context with paralinguistic influences. (See diagram: page 35.)

Recapitulating the linguistic sequence already outlined, we have:

1. A communicational signal detected by one or more of our sense organs (most likely to be our ears and eyes). Then,
2. our auditory and visual reception centres (in the central nervous system) are immediately informed, and,
3. the stimulus is comprehended in the appropriate perception centres.
   But now taking into account the effect of emotion:
4. As we interpret the message received, we may not only critically examine its content, but we may draw on appropriate memories for comparative evaluation. We might indulge in day-dreaming and, depending to what extent our personal sentiments have become involved we shall find that
5. Emotion is engendered.

6. The verbal content of any vocal response that we may contemplate will be organized in the speech centres of the brain, and

7. A vocal response will be uttered accordingly through the mechanism of voice and speech, but our

8. RESPONSE WILL BE EXPRESSIVELY MODULATED AS A RESULT OF VARYING DEGREES OF MUSCULAR TENSION ARISING FROM EMOTIONS AROUSED.

It is from such processes that sensibly linguistic statement becomes dynamic as a result of paralinguistic reinforcement. A balance is preserved. On the one hand, mere semantically precise verbal information (as would emerge from the left-hand path of the chart) is avoided. This kind of speech may be left to producers of science fiction films to dub on to impossibly dispirited 'egg-heads' of the future. Wildly emotional speech is also avoided because the right-hand path is conceived as reinforcing (never usurping) coherent statement of responsible opinion. The means by which utterance becomes nicely significant or discreetly urgent is by the injection of suitable paralinguistic effects, mainly through controlled tonicity, into carefully considered statement.

It is interesting to study the conventional devices of oral communication, on the one hand as rationally expressive of sense, and on the other as paralinguistic reinforcement of such expression.

The way in which we group words into sense-units (conventionally known as phrases), each making its own cumulative contribution to the overall meaning of a complete statement, is clearly a semantic operation, depending upon the lucidity of our thinking. But when our feelings run high, pauses (conventionally referred to as 'dramatic pauses' or 'emotional pauses') interrupt otherwise logically organized groups of words, revealing emotional reactions to the ideas we are expressing.

Intonation, or the melodic patterns to which speech is vocalized, varies similarly in terms of semantic or dynamic classification. Simple inflections are effective means of indicating the suspension or the conclusion of a sense-phrase. Certain kinds of combined inflections have become conventional signs to indicate key-words as they are spoken. But although inflections and intonation may serve mainly a semantic purpose, we all know with what subtlety intonation may express sympathy, compassion, scorn, sarcasm and innuendo in a thousand different ways. As we shall later consider when dealing with pitch, fluctuating emotionally-induced tensions transfer themselves to the speaking voice as the most subtly expressive of all emotionally-expressive melodies.

Stress is particularly noticeable in its range of intensity from the semantic indication of the relative sense-values of words as they are uttered, to the dynamic effect of intense emotional involvement; and stress is perhaps the most obvious of all expressional techniques to explain kinesthetically. Principally effected by increased intensity of voice as the result of breath pressure, and breathing being the most obvious muscularly controlled aspect of voice production, stress clearly results from increased tonicity timed with the key-words of any statement spoken with conviction.

Tone, as generally defined within a practical speech context, is understood to result from hollow cavities in the neck and head acoustically resonating to laryngeal vibration. Vocal tone may be as pleasing to the human ear as a fine violin, or as displeasing as a corncrake. It is not generally realized that, if we were concerned only with the communication of information, a colourless voice would be quite effective as a carrier of distinctly pronounced words, sensibly inflected and stressed. But any modulation of basic tone, arising from a speaker's feelings, adds human interest to the otherwise cold transmission of information. Modulation of vocal tone is brought about by the almost instantaneous transfer to the pharyngeal constrictor muscles of the general tonicity of the body's muscles as a whole. The ready response of the pharynx to emotion was, in the very early days of primitive man, essential to his survival. If he became aware of imminent physical menace, his reflex defence was in petrified immobility and silence. To this day the same response is noticeable in situations of fear – to which many an actor, voiceless at 'curtain-up' on a 'first night' will testify.

Fortunately, the same mechanism works also the other way. The contented sigh at the chance of a well-earned rest derives its tone mainly from a pharynx in a state of relaxation. The muscular responsiveness of the pharynx is important in a kinesthetic theory of dynamic speech because the pharynx is the fundamental resonator of the human voice. The variations of its size and shape, and of the rigidity of its walls, are quite remarkable. Such variations being so emotionally responsive, the pharynx, more than any other of our vocal resonators, is responsible for the rare beauty and the expressive variety of the human voice at its best.

Pace and pitch have utilitarian values in speech. They must be satisfactorily controlled to allow coherence and intelligibility. But each has influence far beyond merely informational needs. Providing neither is taken to such extremes as to cause irritating distraction or unintelligibility, sensitive variety of pace and pitch within oral and auditory limits, plays a significant part in causing others to *want* to listen to what a speaker is saying. Pitch is easy to understand kinesthetically. Because of the conversion of emotion into appropriate tonicity of the laryngeal muscles, pitch rises in frequency as tonicity increases, and falls as tonicity decreases. Not only does this process govern the automatic adoption by a sensitive speaker of a suitable pitch range, but enables him to achieve optimum inflectional expression within that range. Inflection (which we discussed earlier), is, after all, pitch in fluctuation, and may be explained kinesthetically. Mental concentration and emotional intensity are at their strongest in anticipation of a salient point to be made, and both subside when the point has been made.

Consequently, tonicity of laryngeal muscles varies, and the result is that of an inflectional scheme which follows a 'natural' pattern, allowing interesting idiosyncrasies of individual speakers.

Evidence of kinesthetic communication is conclusive. The nervous driver, the authoritarian father, the insecure teacher, extend the stress of their own emotions to all others in their environment as they strive to gain control of their varied situations. More pleasantly, we may observe the 'sense of kinesthesis' through the eyes of a scientist[1] as it 'makes us share the everyday behaviour of others. We know in watching what it feels like to lift a heavy weight, to balance precariously, to make a beautiful stroke at tennis, to skate and to dance.'

[1] J. Bronowski. *The Identity of Man* – Harmondsworth, Pelican.

This same sense may be channelled through voice and speech, extending its influence beyond visual to auditory communication, establishing a *rapport* between speaker and listener unattainable by any merely 'technical' means.

... Dynamic Speech

Kinesthetic improvisation

ABILITY TO RELAX IS THE FIRST ESSENTIAL experience in the acquirement of dynamic speech. Normally, children can relax without difficulty. Adolescents and adults almost always have to learn how to relax. Much has been written on this topic by all kinds of specialists – and by a few cranks! Most of us, it seems, gather useful ideas from a number of sources – from our own experience, from observation of people in general, and (if we are teachers) from experimentation with co-operative pupils.

Relaxation should be conceived as release from tension, but students need confidence to put such a concept into practice. So to get them started, they should learn a routine likely to lead to complete relaxation whenever desired. Described physically, the procedure is a sequence of movements during which a student kneels, sits to one side of his calves, rolls to a comfortable position on the floor – and relaxes. It may be taught in less than half an hour by following clear instructions:

1. Stand easily – bend and straighten the knees – slowly – getting closer to the floor each time. Balance the body by adjusting centre of gravity – mainly by positioning

the torso. Eventually kneel by allowing knees to make
contact with floor – slowly and silently.

2. Kneel – as slowly and silently as possible – by routine
as described. Keeping knees and feet as stationary as
possible, sit on floor – first to one side, then the other,
of the calves. Repeat for practice. Recover, by standing
without using hands.

3. Repeat 1 and 2 as far as sitting by the calves – then
slowly roll in the direction indicated by the sequence,
to a comfortable relaxed lying position.

4. Adjust for maximum relaxation.
Go through this routine frequently (alternately 'right'
and 'left'), beginning dead-slow and increasing the rate
determined by gravity and the mass of the body
falling.

5. When sufficiently supple, *think relaxation* before starting
to collapse.

6. Make final adjustments in lying position for maximum
relaxation.

7. Enjoy relaxation of both mind and body while in the
most propitious condition to do so.

Time spent on perfecting the mechanics of this basic
exercise is justified by the fact that relaxation cannot be
experienced until tension can be abandoned with confidence and, whenever possible, improvisations and 'work-
outs' should conclude with relaxation – as they will have
usually begun with appropriate tonicity. The routine
described may sound disarmingly simple, but the simpler
the means, the more certainly the end – that of complete
relaxation – will be attained. (More complex 'stage-falls'
are, of course, included in an actor's training.)

Environment is an important consideration in regard

to relaxation. Spaciousness, a clean (not over-hard nor slippery) floor, comfortable temperature and quietness (apart from purposive sound) are highly desirable.

Clothing should be such as not to impede free movement, nor cause the wearer any concern.

Suitable music is a most effective inducement to mental tranquillity without which physical relaxation cannot even be envisaged. But quietness is preferable (even to the most soothing music) when once a student has reached the stage of being able to dispel tension by mental recollection of tranquillity from his own perceptive past. The visualization of non-human relaxation at its best (perhaps of a sleek, contented cat), may help a tense person to relax.

Learn to check progress; the teacher by confirming the 'dead' weight of a student's limbs and the looseness of his shoulders, the student himself by consciously ascertaining the degree of relaxation in the various members of his own body. When we are able to will ourselves to relax, we shall have succeeded in acquiring a skill with incidental benefits far beyond those of immediate relevance to our pursuit of dynamic speech.

Tonus is always present in the muscles of the living body, but during relaxation it is reduced to an imperceptible minimum. As muscular tonus is increased beyond this minimum, we may become aware of it in two ways; one (the obvious way) by bodily movement, the other (less obvious) by the impulse to move – referred to in physical culture as 'isometric contraction', i.e. tensing muscles without apparently changing their length.

Exercises for TONUS CONSCIOUSNESS begin with improvisation such as the following, during which awareness of tonus is cultivated by concentrating on the varying intensity of muscular tonicity. Allow the least possible movement of the body or of the part or parts concerned with the significant experience.

1. Lie on the floor. Imagine that you are pleasantly sunbathing. Clouds obscure the sun – you feel chilly – rain begins to fall – you are cold and wet. You look at the sky (it will only be a short shower). The sun breaks through and the rain ceases. You are warm again – and dry. You relax deeply.
2. Adopt a pose as a statue. You have just been modelled out of a plastic moulding compound – you are setting harder – and harder. The sculptor is not satisfied with his work. You feel a solution being poured over you – slowly you soften – slowly you crumple into an amorphous lump on the floor. Relax.
3. Be a hard-frozen snow-man. The sun shines – the warmth penetrates by degrees – you collapse. Relax.

Devise exercises for yourself through which you can stimulate your imagination, develop tonus consciousness, and experience relaxation.

Having become tonus-conscious in a general way, try to discipline your concentration to isolate tonicity to specific parts and areas of the body. Here are some simple exercises.

1. Imagine two bowls of water in front of you; one cold, the other pleasantly warm. (a) Plunge both hands into the cold water. (b) Plunge both hands into warm water. (c) Plunge one hand into each bowl. (d) Reverse the hands in the bowls.
2. Imagine a foot-bath containing warm-to-hot soothing liquid. Your feet are sore from a forced march – so sore that you can immerse them only very gingerly. Once

immersed, they respond to treatment – becoming less sore and, therefore, less tense.
Invent similar exercises.

The next stage, of VOLUNTARILY INDUCED HYPER-TONICITY, has two purposes. One of these is to improve our ability to relax as an instantaneous rebound from extreme tension. The other is to offer initial experience of both extremes – hypertension and relaxation.

Stand and consciously stretch, to their limit, every muscle that you can explore for movement – especially in areas and in directions to which you are unaccustomed. Stretch – stretch – stretch. Then, on your toes, raise the head from the shoulders, thorax from abdomen, torso from legs, arms upward stretch – reach higher – higher. Then relax and (with a fraction of your concentration on the 'fall routine' – until you can do it involuntarily) collapse to relaxation.

FLEXIBILITY AND CONTROL are important in order that members of the body shall respond readily to instructions from the brain. Although exercises for flexibility and control may be concentrated upon specific parts of the body, their intention is that total corporal expressiveness shall not be impeded by reluctant response of any corporate part.

1. Trace a circle, clockwise, in the air with the tip of the right forefinger – moving only the finger itself. After several circles, extend the movement to the hand – (the wrist becoming a 'universal joint'). Extend the movement to the forearm for a larger circle, and finally to the whole arm – from the shoulder.
2. Repeat with the left hand and arm.

3. Repeat 1 and 2 – counter-clockwise.
4. Repeat using both hands and arms in contrary motion.
5. Repeat 4 – reversing direction.
6. Repeat with both hands and arms in same direction.
7. Reverse direction of 6.
8. Experiment with change of time.

Find out from a book on physiology what is happening in bones, joints, tendons, muscles, and nerves, so that, knowing what is taking place, you can close your eyes and see with your mind how it works, especially feeling the muscular control. With your eyes closed test how your kinesthetic sense informs you about movements when they are made without being observed.

Lie on the floor – on your back. Do a similar sequence with feet and legs. Try to co-ordinate right arm and left leg moving in clock-wise circles, while left arm and right leg make counter-clockwise circles! Conclude with con-centration and physiological investigation.

From reputable books, such as *Modern Educational Dance*,[1] you will find as many exercises as you will need for flexi-bility and control of every part of the body. What is important is that you clearly understand the purposes of our particular interest, which are; to understand how we move, to improve our skill in movement, and to develop kinesthetic awareness as the basis of expressive speech and dynamic communication.

Exercises such as those already described should be continued until mastered, and then should give way to imaginatively MOTIVATED IMPROVISATION, the body

[1] By Rudolf Laban. London, Macdonald and Evans.

being used expressively and not merely as an efficiently functioning machine. For example, an exercise for wrist, hand and finger flexibility might be motivated thus:

1. Invent a situation in which it is imperative that you remove from your hands imaginary –
   sump oil,
   dirty water,
   jam,
   grease,
   syrup,
   paste,
   glue,
   with the greatest speed.
2. You have been commanded by a tyrannical emperor to produce a memorial bust of him in an unreasonably short time. Knowing that if you do not produce a good model head for him you will lose your own, you set to work with an imagined lump of clay on a pedestal in front of you.

The aim of the teacher should be to stimulate student creativity, encouraging exercises to be student-directed to the greatest possible extent. Mimes may be worked on a group basis, showing common response to stimulus:

Each student assumes a 'character' in a waxwork tableau. The janitor turns the air-conditioning control the wrong way and it jams. The hall becomes hotter and hotter until all the dummies melt.

Scenes with similar purpose should be devised for automatons, zombies, dolls and so on. Such work, allowing only unified response, reduces possible self-consciousness

D

to a minimum and therefore is useful in instilling confidence.

Group work may also be organized to offer individual
or sub-group response to a common stimulus.

A crowd of starving peasants await the opening of a
ration store. Several leave in search of food elsewhere.
Some decide to smash down the door of the store, while
others run away afraid of becoming involved. A few
collapse with hunger. Some just sit – abject in their
hunger.

Each participant has in that scene the chance of some
individual creativeness within the reassuring 'security' of
small groups showing similar reactions within a common
situation.

There are many opportunities for groups to work in
common situations allowing completely individual responses. One example must suffice.

A ferro-concrete building is in course of construction.
Each 'worker' has a specific task.

Although it is not essential to the purposes at this stage
of development, the organization of 'form' to a strong
climax is very satisfactory. When the climax can be released as an inevitable conclusion to the scene, the ultimate
relaxation is an experience of much profit.

In a jungle clearing, some people are building a 'wattle-
and-daub' kind of emergency shelter. They know that
the weather will break down, but they persevere –
frantically, in spite of their near-exhaustion – some
hewing saplings and fixing them into a rough framework, others mixing mud and slapping it on to the

framework. As they near completion, the storm breaks (on cue from one of the group previously selected) at first with lashing rain, then (on second cue) with a simultaneous 'bolt' of thunder and lightning. They are all thrown unconscious, to the ground.

It is from individual improvisations that a student is likely to experience 'public solitude'[1] from which to develop the ability unashamedly to be himself, poised in his own environment – neither submissive nor arrogant. To begin with, it is a good idea to encourage each student to imagine that his area of the studio is surrounded by partitions, forming a cubicle in which he has complete privacy. The feeling that every other student is similarly confined within the area of his imaginary privacy, allows each to concentrate without the distractions which sometimes intrude at first when classes of students attempt individual work.

Ideas for solo mimes are stimulated every day from a thousand different sources – real life, fiction, in the street, home, office, school, stage plays, the cinema, at church, at the club. Full and varied treatment, and intensity of concentration, can develop the simplest idea into an exciting performance.

Could anything be more commonplace than threading and using a needle and thread? Yet there seems to be no end to the interpretations which may be based on this simple occupation. Try some of the following:

1. Comic. Ham-fisted bachelor. Serious. Working on a vestment. Sentimental. Wedding dress; Christening robe.

[1] A profound and gratifying experience discussed by Constantin Stanislavski in *An Actor Prepares*.

Tragic. A shroud.

2. Situations and Period and Style may range from a Royal Court (embroidery), through a farm worker industriously fastening a bag of corn, or button-holing shirts by sweated labour, to a convict cringingly sewing mail-bags.

3. Add to these factors differences of rhythm and tempo. The excitement of tacking up a hem in order to get to the dance on time, as contrasted with the urgent repairing of a sail before the hurricane reaches full blast; or the age of a seamstress – young and inexperienced, with her mind elsewhere; or senile, with arthritic fingers, wishing she were dead.

Is there any limit to the interpretational permutations of everyday occupations?

There is no precise moment when it becomes desirable for individual expression to become the basis of conscious communication. But a good teacher will allow 'audience situations' to happen as if 'naturally' – allowing the concept to form that the more intense concentration becomes in an individual, the more readily will others be drawn instinctively into mutual absorption with him. Analysed from time to time, this kind of experience leads to an awareness of kinesthetic *rapport* as the real basis of dynamic communication.

Alerting the senses

TOMUS RESPONSE TO IMAGINED SENSORY STIMULUS is important all the time. The student should consider the wise sayings of Stanislavski in *An Actor Prepares*[1] about 'Emotion Memory' through which we are able to remember *how* we *felt* during exciting real-life experiences. Such memories not only vitalize the recollection of the original event, but collectively form, as it were, a reservoir of emotional memories, supplying emotional colour appropriate to the imagined situations of dramatic and poetic literature as the basis of dynamic interpretation of them.

Stanislavski draws a fine distinction between sensation memory (based on sensory experience), and emotion memory of the kind just described. It seems to me that when Stanislavski pointed out that the 'senses . . . are useful, and even important in our art', and that their role is 'for the purpose of influencing our emotion memory' he was implying that zestful sensory experience is indispensable to dynamic communication.

Providing that zestful living has charged the memory with sensory and emotional experience, then our task is to facilitate drawing upon such memory to intensify verbal communication of our own experiences, and for transfer to the interpretation of vicarious experience through drama, prose, and verse. This may be achieved through exercises involving tonus response and emotional reaction to imagined stimulus of the receptor senses, being aware at all times of the vital link through kinesthesis, between impression (whether real or imagined) and expression – basically through appropriate tonicity (on which we shall concentrate for the present), and ultimately through voice and speech (the subject of following sections).

While working on the following exercises, and others which you may create, it is certain that vocal (or even verbal) exclamations will spontaneously break through;

[1] *An Actor Prepares* by: Constantin Stanislavski, London, Geoffrey Bles

this work is therefore highly significant in anticipation of that which follows in which we intentionally cross the border-line between mime and vocal expression.

1. *Sight*

    (a) In a half-light you discern a mysterious object. As you approach it, its appearance evokes a number of extremely different responses.

    (b) You are subjected to a bright 'third degree' glare. It will be fatal for you if you appear to be intimidated. How long can you stand it? What happens after an imagined two hours of gruelling interrogation?

    (c) As a result of a brilliant operation, you are able to see for the first time.

2. *Hearing*

    (a) Listen to a tune. Its identification eludes you. You suddenly remember its title.

    (b) You become aware of a violent quarrel taking place in the next-door flat. You decide to intervene before mischief is done. As you walk past the window you discover that the quarrel is coming from a radio set.

    (c) Trapped underground, you listen for rescuers. You hear sounds of digging – knocking – then voices. The relief is as much as (or more than) you can stand.

3. *Smell*

    (a) Quietly relaxing, you become aware of the smell of gas. It almost overpowers you before you trace its source and deal with the leak.

    (b) An exotic flower has a strong, alluring scent – but it is poisonous. Smell it.

(c) You have some stink-bombs in your pocket with which you intend to play a joke – but your intention back-fires – they get smashed in your pocket.

4. *Taste*
   (a) You are judging home-made wines at a village fête. They vary in taste from vinegar to nectar! Suppose you drink the samples instead of tasting them?
   (b) You are given some fudge by someone you wish to flatter on her cookery. It tastes rancid. You un-successfully try to pretend that you like it.

5. *Touch*
   (a) You think that you can carry a hot dish from the kitchen to the dining-room. Half-way there it turns out to be too hot.
   (b) Scrubbing a floor, you run a splinter into your finger.
   (c) You are attending an invalid who has at last fallen into a long overdue sleep. Mosquitoes settle on his face. Catch them without waking the patient.

Observe kinesthetic indications of tonus experience in others, and note (retrospectively) your own responses.

One habit which should have been formed by now (even in a generally creative setting), is that of concluding improvisations as often as possible with relaxation. This final relaxation should be the natural outcome of the scene itself if it can be dramatically plausible as a release from climactic tension. When this is not possible, then self-directed relaxation should habitually be practised by students for two important purposes; first, to be able to subside (after healthy release of expressional energy) to equally healthy relaxation through which creative energy is replenished; second, to come to know relaxation as the basis of repose – the only background from which dynamic expression can significantly emerge.

Vocal breakthrough

The threshold of vocal breakthrough is variable and largely unpredictable. During early experiences of the sequences already described, there will almost certainly have been vocal, and perhaps verbal, sound spontaneously uttered during what were suggested as 'silent' exercises. Audible breath, inhaled and exhaled through respiratory tracts distended or contracted by emotional stimuli, or because of effort, may well be regarded as the beginnings of dynamic speech. Utterance is always more vital when it overcomes disciplinary restraint.

For most of us, voice and speech-training (in its conventional sense) is essential. But the restricted scope of such training should be recognized. The very important functions of 'routine training in voice production and in orthophonics' is to train the voice to work efficiently, and the speech organs to emit acceptable phonemes. The aim of this course is to offer kinesthetic experience through which efficient speakers may develop expressional resourcefulness in dynamic communication.

Improvisation may offer experience in the transition from ('silent') mime to vocal (not immediately verbal) expression, through scenes evoking gasps, sobs, laughter, giggling, simpering, shrieking (in excitement as well as fear), stertorous breathing (emotional as well as laboured).

Do not manipulate vocal tone, let voice emerge expressively through involvement.

1. The two first arrivals at a social party are inveterate practical jokers. They set a device which 'catches' the other guests as they arrive and who, in turn, join the increasing number of guests waiting for the next 'victim'.

2. A forced labour gang is humping heavy sacks from one place to another. They must not stop until they fall exhausted. Their heavy breathing, grunts, groans, gasps and sobs indicate the emotional and physical stress they suffer until they can work no more – and collapse into oblivion.

3. Celebrities, visiting a chemical factory are overcome by noxious fumes. To make matters worse, the doors (for security) are automatically locked and the only official who knows how to open them is the first to succumb to the fumes.

4. A crowd has gathered to watch firemen rescuing people through the windows of a burning building. You join the crowd and watch as an on-the-spot radio reporter (from whom you take your cues) describes the scene – some are too frightened to be rescued, a pretty typist enjoys being carried in the arms of a strong fireman, a cock-sure exhibitionist tries to descend an escape ladder without help – and falls to the ground, etc.

Verbal follow-up

Considering how long it has taken man to develop speech from the elemental use of voice as non-verbal expression, it is small wonder that we sacrifice so much of our childhood's spontaneity in the frequently frustrating business of learning to speak. As our speech develops intellectually, our problem is to re-charge it with the dynamic vocal intensity which will almost certainly have been reduced (if not entirely lost) as sensibly organized words have become our main (perhaps our only) concern.

I am not at all convinced of the wisdom of jumping direct to 'improvisations involving spontaneous dialogue', although this is frequently recommended. Where this transition has been taken too suddenly, I have often observed an immediate loss of benefits which had accrued from introductory work such as I have already described. I have seen students embarrassed as they have floundered in approaching artificially a skill which had become 'natural' to them in day-to-day conversation. Yet it need not be so if, at this stage more than at any other, we sacrifice everything else to the most smoothly organized transition from the dynamically vocal to the intelligibly verbal.

It is a challenge to devise exercises to bridge with ease this all-important transition. Here is a suggested sample:

The class compiles a list of exclamations, such as:
No!
Help!
Who's there!
Look out!
Stop!
You, up there!
You, down there!
Sit down!
Get out!

Stand clear!
Students organize themselves into groups to create
scenes which are played in ('silent') mime *except for the
exclamation chosen.*

That kind of exercise nearly always succeeds in releasing
the exclamation intelligibly but with the intensity with
which it has become charged during the mime. A similar
exercise allows development of individuality and verbal
responses which, however, need not exceed half a dozen
or so words, such as: 'Fat-bellied pig', 'He's never been
hungry', 'What's the use?' and so on.

A small crowd of serfs are complaining of the cruelty
of their feudal lord when one of their number sees him
approaching. They fall back to allow him to pass. They
plead unavailingly. He passes without apparently
noticing their existence. They utter invectives after he
has gone.

The transition might be taken further in an exercise,
such as the following, in which statement may be extended
without loss of urgency.

Students devise scenes in which the only spoken words
are associated with the climax of the scene which has to be
a statement of some urgency spoken by one of the group
(chosen in advance) to the others. The statement might
be along the lines of: 'Now don't let go of the rope and
we'll all be safe,' or 'The doors will be shut in two
minutes from now; you may leave, or you may stay,
but you must choose.'

Creative interpretation

I am convinced that this is the stage at which the oral interpretation – particularly of drama and verse, but also of suitable prose – should be introduced, NOT TO SUPPLANT THE CREATIVE STREAM OF WORK, BUT TO RUN CONCURRENTLY WITH IT. EACH ASPECT WILL CONTRIBUTE TO THE EFFECTIVENESS OF THE OTHER.

As a link with the previous exercises, and as a creative lead-in to the interpretative stream proper, exercises might incorporate exciting phrases or very short excerpts, from good literature into an otherwise creative mime.

Improvise scenes in which the following excerpts can be included:

> And, listening still, without a word
> We set about our hopeless search.
>
> From *'Flannan Isle'* by W. W. Gibson

> 'Tis ever sweet through pines to see the sky
> Mantling a deeper gold a darker blue
> 'Tis ever sweet to lie
> On the dry carpet of the needles' crown.
>
> From *'Brumana'* by J. E. Flecker

> O to have a little house!
> To own the hearth and stool and all!
> The heaped-up sods upon the fire
> The pile of turf again' the wall!
>
> From *'The Old Woman of the Roads'* by Padraic Colum

> 'Open, for I am weary of the way.
> The night is very black.

I have been wandering many a night and day
Open, I have came back.'

.　　.　　.

'I will not open any more. Depart.
I, that once lived, am dead.'

From 'The Return' by Arthur Symons

Hateful is the dark-blue sky,
Vaulted o'er the dark-blue sea.

From 'The Lotos-Eaters' by Alfred, Lord Tennyson

Halts by me that footfall:
Is my gloom, after all,
Shade of His hand, outstretched caressingly?

From 'The Hound of Heaven' by Francis Thompson

Let us stand here and admit that we have no road.

From 'Homage to the British Museum' by William Empson

I walk, touching the tomb wall with my fingers
In silent entertainment.

From 'Hero Entombed (I)' by Peter Quennell

Through exercises such as those just described, students may be assisted over the first hurdle in their attempts to come to terms with poetry – an adjustment which is becoming urgently necessary for increasing numbers of people who are deficient in speech communicational skills.

Poetry is the most vitally direct language of intense human experience. Because of its power, many are afraid to incorporate anything like it in their day-to-day speech in the prosaic environments in which they are destined to exist – environments which will become even more prosaic as suspicion of all that is poetic deepens. This widespread suspicion (by no means restricted to the illiterate) arises generally from fear of the unknown, and those who are suspicious of poetry are those who are unable to penetrate to the meaning of metaphorical language which, as a result, seems like magic to the uninitiated. When metaphor is also fine-sounding in its words and evocative in its rhythm, a prosaic listener may feel quite alarmed. If he can avoid involvement, he will. If he cannot escape (caught unaware, perhaps, in a recital), he may make derogatory comments to cover his embarrassment.

Any defensiveness a student of speech may reveal towards poetry indicates incomplete adjustment to language. Until such a student matures sufficiently to admit the legitimacy of poetry as heightened expression of intense experience, his everyday speech will lack the emphatic peaks of dynamic communication. For poetry, when once accepted as the only adequate means of describing the reality of human experience, permeates individual language and destroys the artificial barrier often erected between experience and the verbal representation of it. From then on, involvement in poetry and in life become one and the same thing, and poetry becomes the most significant language of the most exciting living.

Immediately you 'let poetry in' you get caught up in the excitement of RHYTHM, finding that in many ways the rhythms of everyday speech are more interesting (because they are infinitely more varied) than the rhythms of verse. Stop for a moment (pom-di-di-pom-pom) and listen to the rhythms (di-pom-di-di-di-pom-di) of what is being said (di-pom-di-pom-di-pom). The rhythmical pattern (di-pom-di-di-pom-di) of each phrase by itself (di-pom-pom-di-di-pom) is fascinating (di-pom-di-di-di), to say nothing (di-di-pom-di) of the variety (di-di-di-pom-di-di) of the rhythmical patterns (di-di-pom-di-di-pom-di) in sequence (di-pom-di). No two alike (pom-pom-di-pom) so far (pom-pom).

The speaking of poetry presents a perfectionist challenge to a student of spoken language. But today the odds are heavily weighted against excellence of achievement in the oral interpretation of poetry.

As children we find delight in rhythm whenever we see or hear it, and we are naturally inclined to speak and move as rhythmically as our inadequately co-ordinated muscles permit. But at some stage, almost, inevitably, adults assume that we must be taught language on the basis of *words*. We are taught to read words, to pronounce words, to spell words, to write words, to consult the dictionary to ascertain the meaning of words – words, that is, in isolation. As the word becomes established as the basic unit of language, our instinctive feeling for rhythm is killed. A word cannot really be rhythmical (nor, for that matter can it make much sense) until it combines with other words into patterns of syllables, stressed and unstressed according to emphasis and pronunciation, resulting in one of the most infectious of all oral communicational devices – rhythm.

Even if our inherent delight in rhythm withstands the onslaught of the 'word-isolationists', there is little less chance of its avoiding devastation from those who appear to recognize what they think is rhythm only after having destroyed it by 'metrically scanning' it. The popular misconception of rhythm as metre has resulted in much so-called rhythmic training being more suitable as military training than as experience likely to lead to sensitive appreciation of rhythm or of its practical development in rhythmical speech fluency.

Occasionally a speech jingle or a rhymed line or two of verse has a regular beat, suitable to its content and entertaining enough to interest children. One such example is A. A. Milne's 'Happiness'.

> John had
> Great Big
> Waterproof
> Boots on;
> John had a
> Great Big
> Waterproof
> Hat;
> John had a
> Great Big
> Waterproof
> Mackintosh –
> And that
> (Said John)
> Is
> That.

Assuming that John is proud of such protection, there is no reason why children should not in imagination stride with him through puddles with a firm beat while saying:

JOHN had GREAT big WATerproof BOOTS on;
JOHN had a GREAT big WATerproof HAT;
JOHN had a GREAT big WATerproof MACKintosh –
And THAT (said JOHN) is THAT.

Verses about clocks and machines and a great deal of doggerel written only to amuse may be treated similarly – with actions accompanying the words.

Occasionally a whole poem is suitably set to an unvarying

metre for special effect. Anyone preparing to speak Rudyard Kipling's:

> We're foot – slog – slog – slog – sloggin' over Africa
> Foot – foot – foot – foot – sloggin' over Africa —
> (Boots – boots – boots – boots – movin' up and down again!)
> There's no discharge in the war! (etc.)

could do worse than 'march' to it for the first run-through, with a view to retaining a sense of military discipline behind the words. But these examples represent the exceptions – in which blatant regularity of beat is used for obvious effect. Far too frequently the beat of poetry is insensitively forced by poetry-through-movement schemes which obscure all subtlety of rhythm by concentrating on metrical beats.

Let us consider one example of a well-known poem, the appeal of which has been destroyed for so many by a heavy-handed (or, more precisely, heavy-footed) approach in class-room 'poetry lessons'. I have myself observed many attempts to interest schoolchildren in William Blake's 'The Tyger', and on many occasions I have shuddered at a use of movement which seems to assume that a tiger is some monstrous mechanically-propelled bulldozer which moves at an unvaried rate over the most diverse terrain, never having to deviate even to a petrol pump, never obstructed in its path, remorselessly moving without motivation. If a non-English-speaking listener were to hear some 'class renderings' of 'The Tyger' that is what (from the stress pattern) he would deduce to be its meaning.

'The Tyger', however, can be excitingly interpreted as a result of kinesthetic carry-over from intelligently organized movement experience – movement which incorporates (in sequence) the supple grace of strong animal

E

sinews, the varying pace through unpredictable jungle, the alert immobility when prey is scented or sighted, the tremendous pounce to the kill, the satisfied somnolence after gorging. This is the kind of kinesthetic experience which will emerge through the rhythms of 'The Tyger' as the basis of its inspired and inspiring poetic comment.

Exercises can be organized intelligently. But rhythm must be allowed to happen instinctively as the result of imagination and intense feeling. Rhythm experienced through movement may be transferred to the speaking of poetry, the movement not considered as having been suppressed, but rather as having been diverted from overt physical expression to vocal indications of responsive tonicity.

Method, of course, must never become stereotyped, but here is a sequence which works well in the use of rhythmical movement as the basis of rhythmical verse speaking.

Thomas Hood's 'The Song of the Shirt' is an interesting example of a basic occupational beat overlaid by variations arising from human tragedy in the environment of 'dark Satanic Mills' (Hood was writing before Blake had died):

(a) Mime stitching with concentration but only occupationally – get the feel of the movement of efficient sewing.
(b) Read the poem, sympathetically, as the basis of involvement in the experience of women subjected to all the evils of sweated labour.
(c) Improvise a scene based on the situation implied in the poem.
(d) Speak the poem, establishing as an undercurrent the tedious regularity of 'Stitch – stitch – stitch' and 'Work

– work – work!', modified by the results of 'fingers weary and worn', 'eyelids heavy and red', 'poverty, hunger and dirt'.

The effect of movement-memory in the speaking of the poem will be quite remarkable. The basic pattern is effective because it stimulates unlimited variety of subsidiary rhythms which jointly communicate a tangible occupational basis of quite dreadful human experience. Experienced in this way, rhythm may be likened to the sea. Tides, as regular as the moon in orbit, great waves and breakers, cross currents and counter-waves, eddies, splashes, ripples, are all related, but although resulting from a common cause, have infinite variety as well as unity.

Without getting into a rut of repetitive method, the approach just described might at least be used as the basis of speaking the following excerpts – and the poems from which they are taken.

Grind of wheels and clank of pumps
Make the thick air twitch and shrink
Like broken nerves, throughout the day.
As dawn throws his torch in the soot-hung sky
An aimless procession shuffles by:
The men march out for another day
Of darkness in the pits below.

.   .   .

Downwards suddenly plunge the cages
From the daylight, to the vast
Abysmal silence of the night:
Now the thick earth holds them fast:
The slaves who sell life for death's wages,
Risking indifferently the blast
Of gas exploding, that choking death.
They tumble into iron carts

Their grimy bodies, as they start,
An echo follows them behind
Through the mean tunnels which drearily wind
Onward and on.
Clanking, clattering, bumping, grinding,
The carts roll through them, onward and on.

From *Coal* by John Gould Fletcher

Staggering slowly, and swaying
Heavily at each slow foot's lift and drag,
With tense eyes careless of the roar and throng,
That under jut and jag
Of half-built wall and scaffold streams along,
Six bowed men straining strong
Bear, hardly lifted, a huge lintel stone.

. . .

What tyrant will in man or God were stronger
To summon, thrall and seize
The exaction of life's uttermost resource
That from the down-weighted breast and aching knees
To arms lifted in pain
And hands that grapple and strain
Upsurges, thrusting desperate to repel
The pressure and the force
Of this, which neither feels, nor hears, nor sees?

From *The Builders* by Laurence Binyon

References have already been made to TONE COLOUR as vocal evidence of emotionally varied tonicity. Paralinguistically, mood is established and atmosphere created more by rhythm than by any other vocal or verbal means. Improvisation is of great help as experience preparatory to the establishment of sensitively appropriate tone in interpretations generally, and in poetry speaking particularly.

(a) Improvise a scene based on tenderness and compassion for animals. If you become really involved, the vocal sounds you make will express your feelings of gentle concern for creatures of nature who are probably much more afraid of us than we are of them. Draw on memories from your own experience as well as from literature and legend – such as 'The Snow Goose' (Paul Gallico) and 'Androcles and the Lion'. If your experience is real, you will be better able to speak:

> If I pass during some nocturnal blackness, mothy and warm,
> When the hedgehog travels furtively over the lawn,
> One may say, 'He strove that such innocent creatures should come to no harm,
> But he could do little for them; and now he is gone.'

(b) Experimenting with rhythms of quiet, simple life close to nature, added to the experience of appropriate tone, will kinesthetically prepare you to speak the whole of Thomas Hardy's 'Afterwards', from which the above stanza was quoted.

Discuss and identify the moods of the following excerpts, and organize improvisational exercises as a basis of interpreting the poems from which they are taken.

> I heard no sound where I stood
> But the rivulet on from the lawn
> Running down to my own dark wood;
> Or the voice of the long sea-wave as it swell'd
> Now and then in the dim-grey dawn;
> But I look'd, and round, all round the house I beheld
> The death-white curtain drawn;
> Felt a horror over me creep,

Prickle my skin and catch my breath,
Knew that the death-white curtain meant but sleep,
Yet I shudder'd and thought like a fool of the sleep of death.

From *'Maud'* by Alfred, Lord Tennyson

I was angry with my friend:
I told my wrath, my wrath did end.
I was angry with my foe:
I told it not, my wrath did grow.

From *'A Poison Tree'* by William Blake

When I am dead, what I have felt so long
    My soul shall know in clearer, purer light:
That where I loathed and hated I was wrong:
    That where I loved and pitied I was right.

From *'Where we are Right and where we are Wrong'* by
Arthur Guiterman

There is a Lady sweet and kind,
Was never face so pleased my mind;
I did but see her passing by,
And yet I love her till I die.

From *'Music of Sundry Kinds'* by Thomas Ford

Soon, at the King's, a mere lozenge to give
And Pauline should have just thirty minutes to live!
But to light a pastile, and Elise, with her head,
And her breast, and her arms, and her hands, should drop
    dead!

From *'The Laboratory'* by Robert Browning

'Twould ring the bells of Heaven
    The wildest peal for years,
If Parson lost his senses
    And people came to theirs,
And he and they together
    Knelt down with angry prayers

For tamed and shabby tigers,
　　And dancing dogs and bears,
And wretched, blind pit-ponies,
　　And little hunted hares.

　　　　　　　　　'*The Bells of Heaven*' Ralph Hodgson

The various ingredients of dynamic speech, especially the instinctual tones and rhythms and the cultivated devices of articulation, do not mix readily – and certainly no more readily by forced stirring.

Movement must expressively develop, and the kinesthetic recalling of it intensify, by constant practice and concentration until tonicity response is consciously perceived at will. The ultimate transfer of kinesthetic awareness to speech is inevitable because it is natural. If we allow it easy access to our language experience it will eventually permeate every significant word we utter, and we become gloriously aware of release from the depth of our personalities through words of our own and of others.

Let us apply kinesthetic methods to four poems as interpretational projects. First, to 'The Discovery' by J. C. Squire.

There was an Indian, who had known no change,
　　Who strayed content along a sunlit beach
Gathering shells. He heard a sudden strange
　　Commingled noise: looked up; and gasped for speech.
For in the bay, where nothing was before,
　　Moved on the sea, by magic, huge canoes,
With bellying cloths on poles, and not one oar,
　　And fluttering coloured signs and clambering crews.
And he, in fear, this naked man alone,
　　His fallen hands forgetting all their shells,
His lips gone pale, knelt low behind a stone,

And stared, and saw, and did not understand,
Columbus's doom-burdened caravels
Slant to the shore, and all their seamen land.

Topics for discussion immediately present themselves. To whom does the earth, or specific parts of it belong? Primitive and civilized life compared. The pros and cons of simplicity and sophistication. Scientific explorers and conquerors. Power domination and possessiveness. Races living defensively alongside each other. Exploitation of ignorance. Racism.

During the kinesthetic experience offered through the following suggested exercises, aim at involvement through strong concentration, allow voice to express as feeling exceeds the bounds of movement, and if you feel like it, develop speech through the improvisations.

Sensory Perception and	*Emotional Response*
– strayed content – gathering shells.	Harmless acquisitiveness.
– heard a sudden strange commingled noise.	Astonishment. Fear of the unfamiliar. Evasive and protective action. Instinctive apprehension.

Rhythm	
Indian who had known no change – strayed content – knelt low behind a stone.	The easy movement of a lonely man, unimpeded by clothes, finding simple pleasure in gathering shells. Change of rhythm to fast withdrawal to cover as the result of alarm.

Improvisations
(a) The 'clambering crews'.   Scene as they sight land.
(b) The Indian.   Solo mime of the Indian
    before he sees the ship,
    and his reactions on seeing it.
(c) The Indian and the ship.   Scene based on the incident.

Interpretation
With your whole concentration on the poem's meaning, and with a general adjustment to suitable initial tonicity, speak the poem, allowing your muscles isometrically to convey your emotions to your voice. Release from sustained tension *after* the last word has been spoken – do not anticipate such release.

(The poem is in the form of a sonnet. Verse speakers with a knowledge of poetic form may allow a sonnet pattern to emerge, providing it is not emphasized – like a garish frame distracting from its picture which would otherwise be attractive.)

'Driving Sheep' (by Rose Macaulay) expresses, in every line, the movement of sheep, with a word or two about the movement of the women driving them, and a startling description of the movement of the sun.

> The green east flows with the tides of the rose
>   Between the bars of night, half-drawn.
> The moon shines cold and faint on the fold
>   Where sheep glimmer, gray in the dawn.
> Oh, thin like a dream their sad cries seem,
>   Caught high above time and space;
> And old as the world, from out fleece dew-pearled,
>   Gazes each meek sheep-face.
> Dazed with sleep, and numb, the sheep-women come,
>   And open the field gate wide.

The sheep surge out in an idiot rout,
  Like gray foam swept on a tide.
Keep steady, move slow, we've three miles to go
  To Grantchester from Chalk Field pen.
Herd them up all the way, lest some go astray,
  Of our imbecile two score and ten.
Unreasoning, blind, each poor unhinged mind
  Takes its thought from the sheep next ahead.
Through each hedge gate (if you reach it too late)
  They charge, wild and pale, like the dead.
Their lilting bleat, their sharp, scuttling feet,
  Are strange, strange as dreams before day,
And ... counting the sheep ... we sway ... into sleep ...
  And trail along ... foolish as they.

The wide tides of gold surge, quiet and cold;
  The green west turns deep blue;
The moon's worn slip very soon will dip,
  Like a pale night-bird, from view,
There seems no sound in the world all round
  But of horn feet and quavering cries
In the young, cold hour ... Like flame, like a flower,
  The sun springs, huge with surprise.

By degrees, the approach should become decreasingly
prescriptive. There is ample stimulus in 'Driving Sheep'
for a whole range of kinesthetic experience. Devise your
own approach to its mood and meaning by any of the
devices already described, and others you may invent, to
culminate in an expressive interpretation.

It should be completely evident by now that kinesthetically sensed impulses to move, channelled through vocal
modulation, are very especially the basis of lyrical interpretation, just as overt movement is a reinforcing device
in dramatic interpretation. Lyrical poems being introspec-

tive, their interpretation demands everything with which tone and rhythm can emotionally charge them. 'Fallen Cities' (by Gerald Gould) is a fine example of sensations arising from external stimulus evoking highly imaginative introspection. In speaking the poem, you may feel tempted to externalize the first and last few lines in order to point the introspective lines between. Well, as an experimental exercise, why not lie on an imaginary beach, toying with sand as described, withdrawing from environment awareness to soliloquize until the mood is broken by the abrupt impact of the external world upon your senses?

> I gathered with a careless hand,
>   There where the waters night and day
>   Are languid in the idle bay,
> A little heap of golden sand;
>   And, as I saw it, in my sight
>   Awoke a vision brief and bright,
> A city in a pleasant land.
>
> I saw no mound of earth, but fair
>   Turrets and domes and citadels,
>   With murmuring of many bells;
> The spires were white in the blue air,
>   And men by thousands went and came,
>   Rapid and restless, and like flame
> Blown by their passions here and there.
>
> With careless hand I swept away
>   The little mound before I knew;
>   The visioned city vanished too,
> And fall'n beneath my fingers lay,
>   Ah God! how many hast Thou seen,
>   Cities that are not and have been,
> By silent hill and idle bay!

But now, and whenever again you *speak* this poem, *only recall your vicarious physical experience kinesthetically*. You, and any listeners who may hear you, will be well rewarded by the results.

For a poem of supreme challenge to kinesthetically based interpretation, I suggest 'Ode to a Nightingale' (by John Keats). It seems to me to have been inevitable that Keats should have written this poem.

It is sensuous, but that is a word that must be qualified. To most people, sensuality implies self-indulgence, sexual promiscuity, bestiality, or lust. Such connotations assume that the only effects of sensory experience are superficial and that the senses offer gratification which is largely physical and therefore, short lived. Keats shows us the outcome of sensuousness when sensory impressions are zestfully apprehended by one of aesthetic sensitivity and almost superhuman imagination.

Perhaps it was not so unfortunate, after all, that Keats had no particular advantages by birth and few by education. The fact that he was eager rather than conscientious as a student, saved his imagination from the stultifying effects of an over-formal education and preserved his superb sensory perceptiveness without which the imagery of his poetry could not have been stimulated. Even his casual approach to medical studies is not without significance. Some lectures may have bored him. On one occasion he said 'the other day during the lecture there came a sunbeam into the room, and with it a whole troop of creatures floating in the ray; and I am off with them to Oberon and fairy-land'. On the other hand, he may well have become aware of the senses as the physical route of experience to the mind, and there is ample evidence of clear understanding of the physical effects of emotion and of the neuro-muscular effects of drugs.

In our present discussion, Keats stands as a supreme example of zestful perception being essential to inspired expression. Of course, the genius quality of his mind linked the one with the other, but then how much more important is keen sensory experience to us ordinary mortals!

In reading 'Ode to a Nightingale' it is impossible at first, I suppose, to escape the mood of melancholy – justified surely by the deep sorrows of Keats. But notice that the nightingale sings of *summer* in full-throated ease, and there is alleviation in a draught of vintage cooled a long age, in dance and song and in sunburnt mirth. It surely is only the transitory nature of what is so sensually gratifying that evokes sadness. But while it lasts and while we can retain alert perception and lively appreciation, let us enjoy living to the full. Yet, when we encounter beauty, there will always be the haunting fear – 'Beauty that must die'.

Read the poem now, subjectively. There is no need to charge it with fussy little explanations of this and that. The whole of its meaning will never be completely clear to anyone. But if you let it by-pass the so-called critical faculties, its truth will engulf you.

> My heart aches, and a drowsy numbness pains
>   My sense, as though of hemlock I had drunk,
> Or emptied some dull opiate to the drains
>   One minute past, and Lethe-wards had sunk:
> 'Tis not through envy of thy happy lot,
>   But being too happy in thine happiness, –
>   That thou, light-winged Dryad of the trees,
>   In some melodious plot
> Of beechen green, and shadows numberless,
>   Singest of summer in full-throated ease.

O, for a draught of vintage! that hath been
  Cool'd a long age in the deep-delved earth,
Tasting of Flora and the country green,
  Dance, and Provençal song, and sunburnt mirth!
O, for a beaker full of the warm South,
  Full of the true, the blushful Hippocrene,
    With beaded bubbles winking at the brim,
      And purple-stained mouth;
That I might drink, and leave the world unseen,
  And with thee fade away into the forest dim:

Fade far away, dissolve, and quite forget,
  What thou among the leaves hast never known,
The weariness, the fever, and the fret
  Here, where men sit and hear each other groan;
Where palsy shakes a few, sad, last gray hairs,
  Where youth grows pale, and spectre-thin, and dies;
    Where but to think is to be full of sorrow
      And leaden-eyed despairs,
Where beauty cannot keep her lustrous eyes,
  Or new Love pine at them beyond to-morrow.

Away! away! for I will fly to thee,
  Not charioted by Bacchus and his pards,
But on the viewless wings of Poesy,
  Though the dull brain perplexes and retards:
Already with thee! tender is the night,
  And haply the Queen-Moon is on her throne,
    Cluster'd around by all her starry Fays;
      But here there is no light,
Save what from heaven is with the breezes blown
  Through verdurous glooms and winding mossy ways.

I cannot see what flowers are at my feet,
  Nor what soft incense hangs upon the boughs,

But, in embalmed darkness, guess each sweet
   Wherewith the seasonable month endows
The grass, the thicket, and the fruit-tree wild;
    White hawthorn, and the pastoral eglantine;
      Fast fading violets cover'd up in leaves;
       And mid-May's eldest child,
The coming musk-rose, full of dewy wine,
   The murmurous haunt of flies on summer eves.

Darkling I listen; and, for many a time
   I have been half in love with easeful Death,
Call'd him soft names in many a mused rhyme,
   To take into the air my quiet breath;
Now more than ever seems it rich to die,
   To cease upon the midnight with no pain,
    While thou art pouring forth thy soul abroad
      In such an ecstasy!
Still wouldest thou sing, and I have ears in vain –
   To thy high requiem become a sod.

Thou wast not born for death, immortal Bird!
   No hungry generations tread thee down;
The voice I hear this passing night was heard
   In ancient days by emperor and clown:
Perhaps the self-same song that found a path
   Through the sad heart of Ruth, when sick for home,
    She stood in tears amid the alien corn;
      The same that oft-times hath
Charm'd magic casements, opening on the foam
   Of perilous seas, in faery lands forlorn.

Forlorn! the very word is like a bell
   To toll me back from thee to my sole self!
Adieu! the fancy cannot cheat so well
   As she is fam'd to do, deceiving elf.

> Adieu! adieu! thy plaintive anthem fades
> Past the near meadows, over the still stream,
> Up the hill-side; and now 'tis buried deep
> In the next valley-glades:
> Was it a vision, or a waking dream?
> Fled is that music: – Do I wake or sleep?

Having made its impact upon you, it will be well worth while examining the poem with a view to communicating it sensitively but dynamically to an audience.

Note the abundance of sensory stimuli implied. 'Drowsy numbness – pains my sense – of hemlock I had drunk – some dull opiate – Lethe-wards had sunk – light-winged Dryad – melodious plot – beechen green – shadows numberless – singest of summer – draught of vintage – cool'd – deep-delved earth – tasting of Flora – country green – dance – Provençal song – sunburnt mirth – beaker full – warm South – blushful Hippocrene – beaded bubbles – purple-stained – drink – leave the world unseen – fade away – forest dim.' Those are enough references to be going along with – from the first two stanzas only. They are all stimuli to emotional response and therefore to varying degrees of muscular tonicity. Some are directly kinesthetic. There are also emotions directly stated – heartache, envy, happiness.

With such profusion of the very stuff from which variety of tone and rhythm are derived, it is inconceivable that, if you intuitively feel the poem and really want to interpret it, you would give a dull rendering of it – unless you are still deficient in the transfer of emotion, through responsive tonicity, to voice.

To become involved in experiences such as those just described is to become convinced that poetry forms a strong, probably the strongest, link between kinesthesis and the spoken word. No doubt this is because of the elemental nature of poetry in terms of mood, rhythm through which mood is expressed, the sensual use of words, and the intensity which results from the concentrated form of poetry. Poetry must have dominated human language in its early days; its primitive use of tone and rhythm must have been part and parcel of common utterance – as indeed they are today in the speech of children before the stultifying effects of over-disciplined language training suppress the initial vigour which is characteristic of the vocal expression of all normal, healthy children.

Moreover, when poetry is predominantly lyrical, the sensitive speaking of it necessitates movement which is kinesthetically experienced but which, instead of being externalized, is transmuted into vocal tones and speech rhythms. Without this internalized movement, the speaking of poetry becomes flat, dull and mechanically metrical – either mere verbalism with neither meaning nor emotion, or artificially modulated voice and speech aiming at the 'poetic effect' of the histrionic elocutionist.

If the right kind of material is selected, the transition to prose interpretation may be easily managed, and the benefits acquired through the meaningful treatment of poetry may be sustained in the language of prose – which need not become prosaic.

The influence of kinesthetic experience is immediately apparent in the following prose excerpts suitable for an improvisational approach similar to that recommended for poetry. Examine each excerpt well, and use the most appropriate of the methods already practised (in poetry) to result in dynamic readings – ultimately without overt gesture, but with vocal evidence of their being kinesthetically experienced.

F

I looked up. The sky was no longer clear. Something like a bank of mist, but shot with quick iridescent flashes, hung over us. Above it, as if through a veil, I could make out one of the strange, fish-shaped craft that I had dreamt of in my childhood, hanging in the sky. The mist made it indistinct in detail, but what I could see of it was just as I remembered: a white, glistening body with something half-invisible whizzing round above it. It was growing bigger and louder as it dropped towards us.

As I looked down again I saw a few glistening threads, like cobwebs, drifting past the mouth of the cave. Then more and more of them, giving sudden gleams as they twisted in the air and caught the light.

Suddenly I realized that all over the clearing men were clawing at themselves, trying to get the stuff off, but where their hands touched it they stuck. They were struggling with it like flies in treacle, and all the time more strands were floating down on them. Most of them fought with it for a few seconds and then tried to run for shelter of the trees. They'd take about three steps before their feet stuck together, and they pitched on to the ground. The threads already lying there trapped them further. More threads fell lightly down on them as they struggled and thrashed about until presently they could struggle no more.

A descending strand wafted across the back of my own hand. I saw some of the strands in front of the cave-mouth hesitate, undulate, and then come drifting inwards. Involuntarily I closed my eyes. There was a light gossamer touch on my face. When I tried to open my eyes again I found I could not. Strands had fallen across my mouth. I could not have opened it to call out if I wanted to. My skin crawled under the touch of the stuff, and the pull of it was becoming painful.

Adapted from *The Chrysalids* by John Wyndham

The black bog had him by the feet; the sucking of the ground drew on him, like the thirsty lips of death. In our fury, we had heeded neither wet nor dry, nor thought of earth beneath us. I myself might scarcely leap, with the last spring of o'er-laboured legs, from the engulfing grave of slime. My enemy fell back, with his swarthy breast (from which my grip had rent all clothing), like a hummock of bog-oak, standing out of the quagmire; and the glare of his eyes was ghastly. I could only gaze and pant: for my strength was no more than an infant's, from the fury and the horror. Scarcely could I turn away, while, joint by joint, he sank from sight.

Adapted from *Lorna Doone* by R. D. Blackmore

It was a foggy day in London, and the fog was heavy and dark. Animate London, with smarting eyes and irritated lungs, was blinking, wheezing, and choking; inanimate London was a sooty spectre, divided in purpose between being visible and invisible, and so being wholly neither. Gaslights flared in the shops with a haggard and unblest air, as knowing themselves to be night-creatures that had no business abroad, under the sun; while the sun itself, when it was for a few moments dimly indicated through circling eddies of fog, showed as if it had gone out, and were collapsing flat and cold. Even in the surrounding country it was a foggy day, but there the fog was grey, whereas in London it was, at about the boundary line, dark yellow, and a little within it brown, and then browner, and then browner, until at the heart of the City – which call Saint Mary Axe – it was rusty-black. From any point of the high ridge of land northward it might have been discerned that the loftiest buildings made an occasional struggle to get their heads above the foggy sea, and especially that the great dome of Saint Paul's seemed to die hard; but this was not perceivable in the streets at their feet, where the whole metropolis was a heap of

vapour charged with muffled sound of wheels, and enfolding
a gigantic catarrh.

From *Our Mutual Friend* by Charles Dickens

Peter dropped feet first into the vertical shaft. He slid to his
knees, edging his legs backwards into the black burrow.
Stooping awkwardly in his tight clothing, he managed to get
his hand under the lintel of the opening and slipped head first
into the tunnel. He waved his legs in farewell, and squirmed
inch by inch along the hundred feet that had taken them so
long to build. Now that it was finished he was almost sorry.
The tunnel had been first in his thoughts for months,
cherished, nursed; and now it was finished and he was
crawling down it for the last time.

He had brought the torch with him and as he inched along
he could see heaps of loose sand dislodged by John's clothing. He noticed all the patches of shoring, strangely unfamiliar in the light but which had been built with difficulty
in darkness.

As he neared the end of the tunnel he flashed the torch
ahead and called softly to John. He was afraid to call loudly
for he was now under the wire and close to the sentry's beat.
He passed the bend where they had altered course and came
to the end of the tunnel.

Where he had expected to find John there was nothing but
a solid wall of sand which was about three feet thick. As he
broke through a gust of hot fetid air gushed out and there
was John, wringing wet with perspiration and black from
head to foot with the dye that had run out of his combinations.
Sand clung to his face where he had sweated and his hair,
caked with sand, fell forward over his eyes. He looked pale
and tired under the yellow light from Peter's torch.

From *The Wooden Horse* by Eric Williams

In the far north-east sky Clare could see between the pillars of Stonehenge a level streak of light. The uniform concavity of black cloud was lifting bodily like the lid of a pot, letting in at the earth's edge the coming day, against which the towering monoliths and trilithons began to be blackly defined.

'Did they sacrifice to God here?' asked Tess.

'No,' said he.

'Who to?'

'I believe to the sun. That lofty stone set away by itself is in the direction of the sun, which will presently rise behind it.'

'This reminds me, dear,' she said. 'You remember you never would interfere with any belief of mine before we were married? But I knew your mind all the same, and I thought as you thought – not from any reasons of my own, but because you thought so. Tell me now, Angel, do you think we shall meet again after we are dead? I want to know.'

He kissed her to avoid a reply at such a time.

'Oh, Angel – I fear that means no!' said she, with a suppressed sob. 'And I wanted so to see you again – so much, so much! What – not even you and I, Angel, who love each other so well?'

He heard something behind him, the brush of feet. Turning, he saw over the prostrate columns another figure; then before he was aware, another was at hand on the right, under a trilithon, and another on the left. The dawn shone full on the front of the man westward, and Clare could discern from this that he was tall, and walked as if trained. They all closed in with evident purpose. Her story then was true! Springing to his feet, he looked around for a weapon, loose stone, means of escape, anything. By this time the nearest man was upon him.

'It is no use, sir,' he said. 'There are sixteen of us on the Plain, and the whole country is reared.'

'Let her finish her sleep!' he implored in a whisper of the men as they gathered round.

When they saw where she lay, which they had not done till then, they showed no objection, and stood watching her, as still as the pillars around. Soon the light was strong, and a ray shone upon her unconscious form, peering under her eyelids and waking her.

'What is it, Angel?' she said, starting up. 'Have they come for me?'

'Yes dearest,' he said, 'They have come.'

'It is as it should be,' she murmured. 'Angel, I am almost glad – yes, glad! This happiness could not have lasted. It was too much. I have had enough; and now I shall not live for you to despise me!'

She stood up, shook herself, and went forward, neither of the men having moved.

'I am ready,' she said quietly.

> from *Tess of the D'Urbervilles* by Thomas Hardy

I saw in my Dream that Christian and Pliable drew near to a very miry SLOUGH, that was in the midst of the plain; and they, being heedless, did both fall suddenly into the bog. The name of the slough was Dispond. Here therefore they wallowed for a time, being grievously bedaubed with the dirt; and Christian, because of the Burden that was on his back, began to sink into the mire.

Then said Pliable, Ah, Neighbour Christian, where are you now?

Truly, said Christian, I do not know.

At that Pliable began to be offended, and angrily said to his fellow. Is this the happiness you have told me of this while of? If we have such ill speed at our first setting out, what may we expect 'twixt this and our Journey's end? May I get out again with my life, you shall possess the brave Country alone for me. And with that he gave a desperate struggle or two, and got out of the mire on that side of the Slough which was next to his own house: so away he went, and Christian saw him no more.

Wherefore Christian was left to tumble on the Slough of Dispond alone: but still he endeavoured to struggle to that side of the Slough that was still further from his own house, and next to the Wicket-gate; the which he did, but could not get out, because of the Burden that was upon his back: But I beheld in my Dream, that a man came to him, whose name was Help, and asked him, What he did there?

Sir, said Christian, I was bid go this way by a man called Evangelist, who directed me also to yonder Gate, that I might escape the wrath to come; and as I was going thither, I fell in here.

But why did you not look for the steps?

Fear followed me so hard, that I fled the next way, and fell in.

Then said he, Give me thy hand: so he gave him his hand, drew him out, and set him upon sound ground, and bid him go on his way.

From *The Pilgrim's Progress* by John Bunyan

Undoubtedly, the widest scope for kinesthetic experimentation is to be found in the interpretation of drama, especially when characterization is unique, situation challenging, and sensory stimulus strong. Examine the following excerpts specifically for these elements and develop vigorous interpretation by imaginative improvisation. It is important to analyse characters (as portrayed by their playwrights) by exploring backgrounds of age, temperament, social class, and so on; and to take into account the conflict or conflicts (internal or external) in which they are involved.

LEAR:

Blow, winds, and crack your cheeks! Rage! Blow!
You cataracts and hurricanoes, spout
Till you have drench'd our steeples, drown'd the cocks!
You sulphurous and thought-executing fires,
Vaunt-couriers to oak-cleaving thunderbolts,
Singe my white head! And thou, all-shaking thunder,
Smite flat the thick rotundity o' the world!
Crack nature's moulds, all germins spill at once
That make ingrateful man!

From *King Lear*; III. ii. by William Shakespeare

JOAN:

Yes: they told me you were fools, and that I was not to listen
to your fine words nor trust to your charity. You promised
me my life; but you lied. You think that life is nothing but
not being stone dead. It is not the bread and water I fear: I
can live on bread: when have I asked for more? It is no hard-
ship to drink water if the water be clean. Bread has no sorrow
for me, and water no affliction. But to shut me from the light
of the sky and the sight of the fields and flowers; to chain my
feet so that I can never again rise with the soldiers nor climb
the hills; to make me breathe foul damp darkness, and keep
me from everything that brings me back to the love of God
when your wickedness and foolishness tempt me to hate
Him: all this is worse than the furnace in the Bible that was
heated seven times. I could do without my warhorse; I could
drag about in a skirt; I could let the banners and the trumpets
and the knights and the soldiers pass me and leave me behind
as they leave the other women, if only I could still hear the
wind in the trees, the larks in the sunshine, the young lambs
crying through the healthy frost, and the blessed blessed
church bells that send my angel voices floating to me on the
wind. But without these things I cannot live; and by your
wanting to take them away from me, or from any human

creature, I know that your counsel is of the devil, and that mine is of God.

From *Saint Joan* Sc. VI by Bernard Shaw

PRIESTS:

My Lord! these are not men, these come not as men come, but
Like maddened beasts. They come not like men, who
Respect the sanctuary, who kneel to the Body of Christ,
But like beasts. You would bar the door
Against the lion, the leopard, the wolf or boar,
Why not more
Against beasts with the souls of damned men, against men
Who damn themselves to beasts. My Lord; My Lord;

From *Murder in the Cathedral* by T. S. Eliot

The very nature of drama causes it to be peculiarly dependent upon sensory experience, the significance of which the playwright may heighten (or at times use for melodramatic effects) by instances of sense deprivation. It is profitable to explore the effects of the loss of each of the senses in turn, in order to realize the compensations made by the senses which remain alert, and to confirm the absolute dependence of them all upon the kinesthetic sense for their manifestation in expression and communication. One such project, as an example, could deal with blindness. Several instances come immediately to mind.

In *Oedipus*, the king puts out his own eyes in horror of his crimes. (The Seneca version being more theatrical than that of Sophocles.) In Shakespeare's *King Lear*, the Earl of Gloucester, suspected of treachery, has his eyes put out by the Duke of Cornwall. In a play *Autumn*, adapted by Margaret Kennedy and Gregory Ratoff from the Russian by Ilya Surguchev, a barrister is temporarily blind during ophthalmic treatment. The father in *The Paragon*, by Roland and Michael Pertwee is blind throughout the play. In *Winter Sunshine*, by G. A. Thomas, a confidence-trickster pretends to be blind while on a pleasure cruise.

The improvisational approach to drama needs to be applied intelligently, for there is always the risk of liberated expression becoming extravagantly histrionic. Kinesthetic transfer of movement to voice and speech may be facilitated by the careful selection of exercises graded from those which imply release of dramatic intensity largely through movement, to those in which communication without visual distraction is essential, for example as in a descriptive atmosphere-setting prologue:

CHORUS

Now entertain conjecture of a time
When creeping murmur and the poring dark
Fills the wide vessel of the universe.
From camp to camp through the foul womb of night
The hum of either army stilly sounds,
That the fix'd sentinels almost receive
The secret whispers of each other's watch:
Fire answers fire, and through their paly flames
Each battle sees the other's umber'd face;
Steed threatens steed, in high and boastful neighs
Piercing the night's dull ear; and from their tents
The armourers, accomplishing the knights,
With busy hammers closing rivets up,
Give dreadful note of preparation:
The country cocks do crow, the clocks do toll,
And the third hour of drowsy morning name.
Proud of their numbers and secure in soul,
The confident and over-lusty French
Do the low-rated English play at dice;
And chide the crippled tardy-gaited night

Who like a foul and ugly witch, doth limp
So tediously away. The poor condemned English,
Like sacrifices, by their watchful fires
Sit patiently and inly ruminate
The morning's danger, and their gesture sad
Investing lank-lean cheeks and war-worn coats
Presenteth them unto the gazing moon
So many horrid ghosts.

From *Henry V*, IV, i by William Shakespeare

If gesturing be considered redundant to writing so graphic
as that, it certainly would destroy the lyrical qualities of:

ROMEO

But soft! what light through yonder window breaks?
It is the east, and Juliet is the sun!
Arise fair sun, and kill the envious moon,
Who is already sick and pale with grief,
That thou her maid are far more fair than she:
It is my lady; O, it is my love!
O, that she knew she were!
She speaks, yet she says nothing: what of that?
Her eye discourses, I will answer it.

JULIET
Ay me!

ROMEO
She speaks:

O, speak again, bright angel! for thou art
As glorious to this night, being o'er my head,
As is a winged messenger of heaven
Unto the white-upturned wondering eyes
Of mortals that fall back to gaze on him,
When he bestrides the lazy-pacing clouds
And sails upon the bosom of the air.

JULIET

O Romeo, Romeo! wherefore art thou Romeo?
Deny thy father and refuse thy name;
Or, if thou wilt not, be sworn my love,
And I'll no longer be a Capulet.

ROMEO

Shall I hear more, or shall I speak at this?

JULIET

'Tis but thy name that is my enemy;
Thou art thyself, though not a Montague.
What's Montague? it is nor hand nor foot,
Nor arm, nor face, nor any other part
Belonging to a man. O, be some other name!
What's in a name? that which we call a rose
By any other name would smell as sweet;
So Romeo would, were he not Romeo call'd,
Retain that dear perfection which he owes
Without that title. Romeo, doff thy name,
And for thy name, which is no part of thee,
Take all thyself.

ROMEO

I take thee at thy word:
Call me but love, and I'll be new baptized;
Henceforth I never will be Romeo.

From *Romeo and Juliet*, II, ii by William Shakespeare

Reflective soliloquy brings us to the ultimate in transfer of
the mental and emotional direct to and through voice and
speech while movement is restricted to facial and postural
response to tonicity. Not until the processes which govern
the kinesthetic transfer of mental and emotional concentration to voice and speech are reliable and spontaneous, can
a speaker hope to communicate the subjective intensity of:

LADY MACBETH

Come, you spirits
That tend on mortal thoughts, unsex he here
And fill me, from the crown to the toe, top-full
Of direst cruelty! make thick my blood,
Stop up the access and passage to remorse,
That no compunctious visitings of nature
Shake my fell purpose, nor keep peace between
The effect and it! Come to my woman's breasts,
And take my milk for gall, you murdering ministers,
Wherever in your sightless substances
You wait on nature's mischief! Come, thick night,
And pall thee in the dunnest smoke of hell,
That my keen knife see not the wound it makes,
Nor heaven peep through the blanket of the dark,
To cry 'Hold, hold!'

From *Macbeth*, I. v by William Shakespeare

An imaginative technological device – in an age of dubious gimmickry – is worth noting because it so clearly demonstrates the ideal in soliloquy. In a film, the audience was able to *hear* the recorded soliloquy of Hamlet (played by Sir Laurence Olivier) while seeing him obviously in the throes of intellectual uncertainty, but apparently producing audible words (which were recorded) direct from his mind – without recourse to physical voice and speech. How near can you (unaided by the facilities of microphone and cine-camera) get to this ideal?

From my own experience and observations, I am convinced that, apart from immediate invigoration of interpretational speech skill, the benefits I have described are carried over into our everyday speech, not destroying its spontaneity, but influencing its quality and strengthening its effectiveness.

How do we know when the method is working? Let us take the case of a radio actor who has to die in a melodramatic situation. The set-up may be that he is supposed to take an overdose of a powerful sedative, and that he has to mutter some lines – important to the plot – before a final groan and ultimate collapse. The actor, of course, supplies only the voice and speech; the clink of the glass, the shuffle of feet, and the thud of the falling body (a sack of sand), will be organized by the sound-effects team. The co-ordination of dialogue and sound-effects may be meticulously well timed, but the scene will not sound convincing unless the actor is able convincingly to reproduce vocally the impression of emotions and actions prescribed in his script. His ability to do so is dependent upon his kinesthetic sensitivity.

Effectiveness of speech communication in non-theatrical situations depends upon the same premise. When we are genuinely involved in discussion, kinesthesia happens automatically. When we are able more formally to speak effectively in less spontaneous circumstances, we can assume that we are using kinesthetic processes, either consciously being acquired while learning, or as the result of habits which have been consolidated during the systematically organized experiences of a kinesthetically-based course of training.

When we respond in muscular tonicity appropriately to thoughts and feelings and when, desirous of communicating them, the effects of such response are significantly expressed in voice and speech, only then have we the capacity to speak with maximum effectiveness.

Significant everyday speech

We now approach the stage which, for most of us, should be the most profitable of the course in terms of practical benefits. Very generally stated, we aimed first at spontaneous release of expression through movement, voice and speech. We then set about injecting a similar kind of creativity into the interpretation of suitable literature, hoping to gain oral language experience of the highest quality. As we became involved at depth in our interpretations, improved expressional skills would have penetrated our everyday speech habits. The cycle is theoretically complete, but it may be developed from a circular movement on a horizontal plane to helical projection vertically. This concept is, to my mind, of extreme importance. If a student is forced to linger too long at any one stage, boredom will destroy all chances of further progress. He should be encouraged to complete the cycle at a pace consistent with both effective learning and the stimulus to proceed to further learning. He should be urged to pursue the cycle again and again, each time on a higher plane, striving for excellence.

In a well-integrated speech course, practice, theory and technique are organized on the assumption that each aspect is dependent upon the other two. Under competent guidance, students will be encouraged constantly to discuss their experiences, and in addition to the obvious intellectual benefits of such discussions, hidden assets are acquired, not least of which is the automatic carry-over into conversation of expressional skills acquired purposefully during organized exercise. A teacher who can organize smooth transitions from interpretational projects to immediate discussion about them is already well on the way towards ensuring that what is acquired by his students in the class-room will eventually permeate their personalities in other, more general, situations. But a conscientious teacher is almost certain to want to extend these effects through controlled teaching to the complete consolidation of useful habits and sound attitudes.

Stated negatively, little carry-over (if any) can be expected from 'recitation' to everyday speech; only artificiality could be anticipated from the sporadic application of superimposed techniques.

Positively stated, everyday speech will benefit from organized training, as naturally as surrounding sand becomes saturated with water from a stream flowing through it, if progressive development of expressiveness is acquired by intense involvement in the interpretation of evocative writing, and if exercises are creatively organized to propitiate the transfer of expressional skills from interpretation to spontaneous utterance. The devising of such experiences to stimulate creative speech without reliance either upon the words of playwright, novelist or poet, or upon predetermined statement, challenges the inventiveness of teacher and student to the utmost. If this stage is imaginatively dealt with, the student's everyday communication will benefit by the unconscious infiltration of abilities acquired from the improvisational interpretation of suitable scripted material.

In approaching this consolidational phase, we should keep well in mind the sequence of experiences which should have preceded it. There would at first have been improvisational experience to intensify sensory awareness – in particular, the consciousness of kinesthetic sensation, and the transfer through kinesthesia to a wide range of expression through voice and speech. Through the oral interpretation of suitable written material, the various components of expression would have been acquired; and so long as the treatment was creative, techniques would have developed unconsciously.

If these processes have been understood and accepted, some improvement may have taken place in our everyday spontaneous speech, but we still have to consolidate the carry-over. Speech significance has much to do with content and, even disregarding the conditioned response to casual salutations, and redundant comments on the weather and comparatively unimportant news, we shall almost certainly feel some frustration as we consciously discard the scripts of literary geniuses and attempt to charge our own, less inspired, ideas with communicational intensity, not supercharging with hypocrisy the expression of inferior ideas, but stating with integrity and conviction that which we honestly believe.

Continuity with previous work under 'Vocal break-through' and 'Verbal follow-up' may seem to have been broken, but it is only apparently so. The improvisations, which were designed to lead to expressive (mainly excla-matory) utterance, paved the way towards the meaningful interpretation of imaginative ideas stated in well-organized language. Now, with the facility of expression which has thus been gained, it is suggested that we employ such impro-visations as the following, to help us over our last hurdle.

Have a tape recorder ready so that you may discuss the speech that emerges from these improvisations, and from others that you will devise for yourselves.

1. Lonely, in your room, you are alerted by a stealthy noise outside. You are convinced that someone is trying to pick the lock of your door. Frightened, you

G

move quietly to the telephone and dial the emergency number. A policeman (another student) answers the phone. You explain your suspicion to him and, after he has taken your name and address and has promised to send help, you ring off. Almost immediately, you hear a miaou and you confirm that outside your door there is nothing more menacing than a stray cat. You ring the police again, hoping that a squad car has not already left.

An improbable situation? Nevertheless, listen to the recording and accept the assessment of the group as to the general convincingness of both speakers. Could it conceivably have been a real call? If not, why not? Was fear at first communicated by the caller's tone-colour, interrupted rhythm, urgency of pace, intensity, and so on? Was release of fear, or perhaps embarrassment, or amusement, communicated in the second call? What were the policeman's reactions – did they sound convincing? Assess, in this general way, speech evoked by other situations organized to become increasingly probable.

2. In an area too isolated to be served by a regular ambulance system, someone for whom you are responsible needs immediate conveyance to hospital. You dial the local one-man-hire-car owner who makes a number of excuses to avoid becoming involved. In the end you persuade him to help.

3. You are returning a library book which had been defaced before you had borrowed it. The librarian, now noticing it for the first time, accuses you.

4. You have inadvertently posted two letters each in the wrong envelope and your carelessness could have serious consequences. You try to persuade the postman, collecting the mail from the post box, to let you

have your letters back. But he has clear instructions not to do so.

5. During a wave of car thefts, you are trying innocently to open the door of someone else's car which is identical with your own. A detective approaches you.

Acting out human relation situations offers every chance of involvement by those participating. Situations which you have heard of in the lives of others will give you ideas for situations which you might envisage happening in your own experience.

6. Your wife (or husband) has arranged to go out for the evening on which you regularly do so. One of you must stay at home unless you can get a baby-sitter.

7. Your neighbour is very enthusiastic about the glory of his willow tree, but its roots are interfering with your drains.

8. You have welcomed a relation to stay in your house as a guest. The welcome wears thin after several weeks because of noisy visitors he brings home and who frequently stay until the small hours of the morning.

9. A door-to-door caller tries to persuade you that the organization he represents holds the solution to all world problems.

10. You are a member of a church with whose beliefs you agree with one exception. You argue your case with another member who does not share your objection.

11. Conventional parents are concerned with their children's participation in protest marches.

12. Your boss, whose patronage you feel is unwise to ignore, asks you to help in the local organization of a political party whose policy is entirely opposed to your own convictions.

Giving instruction is a frequent speech necessity and almost as frequently implies a kind of speech devoid of impact. Try to instruct interestingly by choosing topics about which you have enthusiasm strong enough to make you want to share. If starch upsets your stomach, you are not likely to evoke much interest in explaining how to make a cream cake! But if your main hobby is gardening you should be able to send your audience away not only able to start a compost heap, but impatient to get going. So, depending upon your own interests, choose instructional topics such as:

Making a (musical) recorder,
Carving balsa wood,
How to waterproof a jacket,
Making an aquarium,
How to glaze a broken window,
Re-upholstering an old armchair,
A first exercise in bookbinding,
Weaving,

trying to communicate delight in the experience which qualifies you to instruct. In much creative and constructional instructing, there are special opportunities for the communication of kinesthetic memories; the feel of clay, the weight of metal, the muscular control needed for wood-turning, and so on.

Similarly, in situations in which a professional or near-professional standard of speech is appropriate, and specific skills, such as those required in giving an address or taking part in forum or debate, are essential, choose only topics which are dear to your heart. Theories of speech-making, rules of debate, and procedural formalities, so often become the main concern of would-be effective speakers;

but by themselves do nothing to ensure persuasive communication unless the speaker is able to transfer his feelings through muscular tonicity to voice and speech.

Assessment is important not only for its obvious purposes of gauging ability and analysing causes of unsatisfactory progress, but also as stimulus to the kind of listening by which understanding is finally reached of the vocal agencies through which ideas and feelings are expressed through kinesthetic transfer.

General assessment naturally must precede analytical assessment. A simple screening check may be made of the members of a class by gathering their general impressions about each other in turn as they speak on topics in which they are interested. The following format is all that is required.

LISTENER'S NAME........................ DATE............						
As you listen to each member of your class in turn, ask yourself the questions as indicated. If your answer is 'yes', put a (+) in the speaker's column. If your answer is 'no', put a (—). If you are uncertain, leave the square blank.						
Identification of speakers:						
Does the speaker arouse my interest?						
Does the speaker hold my attention?						
Do I believe him to be sincere?						
Would I (on my own initiative) listen to him again?						

If 2 marks are allowed for each 'blank' and 5 for each (+), a teacher should not find it too burdensome to calculate a percentile rating for each student's general speech effectiveness in the opinion of his peers.

Obviously, the less effective a speaker is, the more urgent becomes an analysis of the causes of his ineffectiveness. Certainly students who score lower than 75 per cent have room for the kind of improvement that will be achieved best by attention to their particular weaknesses. To organize remedial work efficiently, analytical assessment is essential. Before we attempt analytical assessment, we need to be quite certain of our ability to isolate each of the various components which combine to make speech dynamic. A word or two about each factor is timely at this stage.

Assessing BASIC VOCAL TONE depends upon judging its adequacy and quality as the carrier of articulate speech. Is it too weak to support its phonemic signals; or is it over-loud, competing disastrously with clear enunciation? Is it pleasant or unpleasant to listen to? There is much less difference between individual vocal organs than between the way they are used or abused. No speaker should be excused from producing optimum basic tone from his particular vocal mechanism as the result of efficient tonicity.

TONE COLOUR is a useful name for the modification of basic tone to communicate a speaker's feelings as they vary from the mood of one situation to another; constantly fluctuating during sustained communication. A listener must ask himself whether the speaker's tone becomes static (even if his voice is pleasantly toned, a speaker who is concerned only with demonstrating the attractiveness of his voice is usually a bore), or whether his tone changes meaningfully, indicating his attitudes to, depth of involvement in, and sentiments for, the content of his discourse.

By INTENSITY is meant the effect upon movement, voice and speech of that degree of tonicity appropriate to the situation and content. Usually there is an intensity norm for each particular occasion, with fluctuations resulting from a speaker's involvement in his subject, and the reactions of his audience. Before he begins to speak, a speaker communicates kinesthetically with his audience as a result of posture; and if his posture is a natural outcome of tonicity, the tone colour of his voice and the firmness of his enunciation will consolidate initial communication. To assist analytical assessment, a listener might also observe whether slackness or over-tenseness of posture seems to indicate hypotonicity or hypertonicity; either symptom is almost certain to weaken communication.

In judging STRESS we should ask ourselves whether words are given specific degrees of intensity in proportion to their sense values. EMPHASIS is the manifestation of significance in a general kind of way and has much to do with CLIMAX. Sensitive emphasis keeps an entire inter-pretation or extemporaneous speech in balance as to its effect upon an audience, while climax – resulting from the progressive intensification of all available expressional devices – automatically compensates for the natural tend-ency of audience-interest to wane after the initial impact has been made.

PACE is more complex than most speakers and listeners imagine. The intellectual content of what is being delivered must have a strong bearing upon the rate of its delivery. Profound thoughts cannot be absorbed at so fast a rate as trivialities can be dealt with. The intellectual, cultural and social levels of audiences need to be considered by a speaker whose rate of utterance must not outstrip the receptivity of those with whom he would communicate. The size of an auditorium, its acoustics, and the size of an audience irrespective of the room they are in, as well as the articulatory agility of the speaker, all have bearing upon the ideal pace in the circumstances. Pace norm is therefore difficult to determine and if established would not be very profitable. For those interested, a rate of 160 words per minute is a figure worth noting. Ideal rate, however, is governed by a speaker's natural involvement in what he is saying, modified to suit situational conditions. So we ask, is the speaker's pace compatible with the mood and intellectual content of his subject? Is it not too fast for his articulatory control? Does it take into account the audience's degree of receptivity? Is it suitable for the situation in which we find ourselves?

In discussing real pace, we intentionally omitted reference to the illusion of pace, because this brings us to a consideration of RHYTHM which may change the apparent tempo of speech without increasing or decreasing its actual rate in terms of words per minute. Rhythm in the speaking of verse should be readily perceived, but may also be assumed from the establishment and communication of atmosphere and mood, for rhythm shares with tone-colour the responsibility or the oral realization of a poet's intentions in these respects. Rhythm in the speaking of prose is more elusive, and can be assessed only by appreciation of the effect caused by the ever-changing rhythmical patterns of successive phrases – a phenomenon which we have considered elsewhere.

PHRASING needs to be sensible. To assess skill in phrasing, we need only to decide to what extent thought is expressed in spoken sense units each of which adds cumulatively to the communication of a sequential mental structure. Except for very occasional rhetorical effect, phrases must not be redundant, and a speaker should be penalized for lack of discipline in this respect.

PAUSES separate phrases and need to be sustained long enough to allow the preceding phrase to be understood and assimilated by the listener, while the speaker mentally organizes the following phrase.

INFLECTION carries continuity through phrases and also through pauses which would otherwise tend to separate phrase from phrase, and may be assessed by deciding how clearly a speaker is able to indicate suspension and establish conclusion as he intends. INTONATION is structured by inflections in continuity. A sensitive speaker uses intonation and compound inflections together to express subtle shades of meaning.

PITCH is governed by a speaker's involvement in the meaning and emotion of his utterance, but is restricted to his vocal range. A listener may ask himself whether a speaker's pitch line does in fact communicate tonicity derived from his involvement and not reveal tension resulting from poor adjustment to the situation.

It has been a basic assumption throughout this book that we are concerned only with a method of expression and communication through movement, voice and speech, and not with physical training, voice production and enunciation as such. Therefore we are not concerned with students who have basic postural, vocal and phonemic problems, other than to note that until the basic instruments of expression are capable of making audible and intelligent speech sounds, they cannot effectively communicate by oral-aural means. Therefore, for a student who is considered unsatisfactory as a result of the first general screening, a test of basic voice and speech is recommended. This may be a simple consensus of opinion on his audibility and intelligibility, or a more complex scheme such as might be used by speech therapists and experimental phoneticians, but it is essential through some such test to confirm whether or not the general ineffectiveness is the result of inadequate voice production or inefficient speech formation. For the present we will concede two preliminary sections on voice and speech in an assessment otherwise related exclusively to expressiveness. It is almost certain that if a student scores low ratings in these two areas, he is unlikely to score high ratings in other areas; in fact the validity of a particular assessment might well be checked on this basis, for it is quite certain that high evaluation of other factors would be inconsistent with low evaluation of the first two factors.

LISTENER'S NAME........................ DATE...........					
As you listen to other members of your class in turn, ask yourself the questions as indicated. Put a (+) if your answer is 'yes', and a (−) if your answer is no. If you are doubtful, leave the square blank.					
Speakers' identifications:					
Is the speaker's *voice* adequate in terms of volume?					
Is the speaker's *speech* intelligible?					

Phrasing. Does each phrase add specifically, and without waste of words, to the whole sequence of ideas?						
Pausation. Am I given time to evaluate the content of each phrase?						
Inflection. Do I receive clear indications as to whether an idea is suspended during a pause or whether a thought sequence is complete?						
Intonation. Is speech melody meaningful in that its change of pitch indicates degrees of significance?						
Rhythm. Do the stresses, placed primarily for meaning, also form agreeable rhythmical patterns?						
Pitch. Is the pitch indicative of tonicity response while also being neither too high nor too low to allow easy modulation?						

Basic vocal tone. Is the speaker's voice free from harshness resulting from muscular tension?						
Tone colour. Is the basic tone modulated by variable tonicity arising from the speaker's reactions to his subject matter?						
Intensity. Does the speaker's overall tonicity, as shown by posture and heard in voice and speech, indicate suitable adjustment to situation?						
Stress. Is stress allocated to key words only?						
Emphasis. Is significance established by sensitive tonus reactions transferred to voice and speech?						
Climax. Does significance increase as the speaker proceeds?						
Pace. Does the speaker mentally and emotionally carry me along with him?						

Time spent in collating information about students who are not generally satisfactory, but who appear to have reasonable voice and speech quality, is always well spent. Simple analysis of the assessment is the only scientific basis for the prescription of suitable exercises in areas needing specific attention, or of more background work, as appears to be required. If suitable work is carefully organized on the basis of careful diagnosis, the final goal will be sooner and more effectively reached. The goal? That speech will always be ready to emerge with an expressiveness appropriate to the situation.

Problems and principles

If we wish to master the art of speech, it is as well that we should recognize such problems as may obstruct our effort and consider such principles as may assist us in our progress.

A serious obstacle arises from the general reluctance to take a realistic view of the significance of emotion upon effective speech.

It should be obvious that emotion is still the driving force of human communication – even in the twentieth century. Such an assumption is amply supported by social workers, psychologists and historians. Yet, the frequent abuse of emotion in today's world is breeding a negative attitude which attempts to suppress the expression of feeling instead of encouraging its release through legitimate outlets, such as dynamic speech. In balanced speech (with thought and feeling complementarily poised emotion will convey ideas in an elementally propelled vehicle. Thoughts may thus be excitingly expressed, and emotion wholesomely released. Instead, there is today an over-concern with verbal statement in which semantics and psycho-linguistics dominate language study, restricting language almost entirely to the intellect.

We cannot ignore the influence of computors. Arranged to deal precisely with exact informational data, the computor answers questions which the human brain finds it difficult to formulate! This may be useful, providing science-fictional exaggerations of 'electronic brains' do not captivate the fancy of the man in the street to the extent of his seeing the ideal human mind similarly concentrating exclusively on the logical analysis of received information and directing its body as an emotionless robot.

To make matters worse, those cultural areas classed under the general heading of aesthetics, and which once held high prestige in liberal education, have swung violently away from their traditional recognition of the importance of emotional maturation. The brain makes mental exercises of what were once emotional experiences. The appeal of much modern poetry is intellectual, frequently serving less purpose than prose on a mental plane, and defeating its more valid purposes on an emotional plane.

The denial, in our present-day approach to oral language of the significance of its instinctual basis, is very disturbing; for it is the almost exclusive concern for sense content, and the defensive abhorrence with which emotional colouring tends to be regarded, that is sapping from today's speech the energy which converts sensibly conceived ideas into dynamically communicative speech.

William James put it: '. . . our emotions are mainly due

to those organic stirrings that are aroused in us in a reflex way by the stimulus of the exciting object or situation. An emotion . . . is not a direct effect of the object's presence on the mind, but an effect of that still earlier effect, the bodily commotion which the object suddenly excites; so that, were this bodily commotion suppressed, we should not so much feel fear as call the situation fearful; we should not feel surprise, but coldly recognize that the object was astonishing'.[1] Whether or not James's ideas in general deserve the scant regard accorded them by many modern psychologists, his differentiation between being aware of, and experiencing, emotion, is very illuminating in our present discussion.

Applied to at least two areas which concern us, acting and verse-speaking are too frequently approached with a consciousness of sensory imagery, but without the feeling of sensory experience, to the detriment of drama and poetry.

The right kind of training cannot begin early enough in the life of the individual providing it is understood that it consists, in the early years especially, of setting up the right kind of environment and giving the right kinds of opportunity to pupils, rather than over-organizing prescriptive schemes. Children, for instance, find instinctive delight in movement – (testy old people sometimes wish they did not!) Their imagination is usually lively. They are excitingly creative. They experience, day in, day out, all degrees of muscular tension. So long as they are allowed to enjoy a healthy physical and psychological environment, we can assume that they will vigorously express themselves

[1] 'The Gospel of Relaxation' from *Talks to Teachers of Psychology: and to Students on Some of Life's Ideals*, by William James, London, Longmans, Green.

and communicate as an exciting part of normal life. Were it not for the fact that amicable communal life necessitates some individual social adaptation, the ebullient speech of children would develop quite naturally into dynamic oral communication on an instinctively kinesthetic basis without instruction or direction – merely with guidance and encouragement from enlightened teachers who understand the natural development of speech from movement. Organized training in oral communication seems first to be needed when children *become aware* of externally applied discipline (which is not necessarily when it is first applied). The more subtly children are made aware of their social obligations, on the basis of consideration for others, the more likely their resultant self-discipline will render suppressive discipline unnecessary.

Sensibly organized oral language training should be regarded as an antidote to all that is unhealthy in modern communications, the symptoms of which may be verbosity, shyness, uncouth aggressiveness or apathy, all of which social disadvantages may be alleviated by the gratification of confident speech. With these assumptions, let us briefly consider an applied course based on the principles already discussed.

On a purely physiological basis, the mechanisms of the body must be resilient if they are to lead to kinesthetic sensitivity. No lesson should proceed, in fact no day should pass, without a zestful period of physical exercise designed to offer sheer delight in healthy awareness of the human physical organism. Each student should be urged to explore the full range of individual movement, and the ever surprising permutations which emerge from experimentation with group movement.

It is not necessarily a sign of negative thinking to call

attention to the physical tensions which are prevalent in our time. We need to approach relaxation realistically as a positive antidote to an admitted problem. Students who are habitually tense will remain expressionally inept until their tensions are reduced at least to the level of efficient tonicity.

Therefore, limbering for flexibility, exploration of the body's resourcefulness, experience of tonus (from relaxation to hypertonicity) and the establishment of individual tonicity norms, should be integrated into the preliminary section of each work period. There should be similar opportunities for vocal exploration and liberation when (regardless of 'techniques') students are encouraged to vocalize; the more unusual the sounds the better! As the work develops, voice will tend to relate itself to muscular effort – clearly indicating the naturalness of the relationship between tonus experienced and resultant vocal tone produced.

Group and individual improvisations should play a significant part in any course intended to lead to dynamic communication. Improvisation adds imaginative motivation to the physical experience of the limbering sections. Then we should have stretched the resources of the body to their maximum; now we stretch the resources of the imagination – which have no limit. Through graded improvisation we offer opportunities to experience in true sequence the psychological processes of dynamic expression. Great stress should be laid upon sensory perception and imagery. Emotions are experienced as the outcome of stimuli received and interpreted as a result of accumulated individual experience. Voice and speech break through with impact. The true foundations of dynamic speech are laid.

H

An imaginative teacher will watch for the right moment to introduce interpretative exercises, so that the spontaneity of the creative experience will be retained in the re-creation of suitable literature. It is improbable that the writings of dramatists, novelists or poets will be brought to life other than by readers who are able to draw upon a wide range of their own creative experiences and who, in fact, can devise suitable improvisations to penetrate imaginatively into the subject matter to be interpreted. The interaction between creative and interpretational work is extremely profitable to all students of practical speech. The spontaneity which gives life to improvisation may be carried over into interpretational reading, speaking or acting, while techniques experimentally acquired from interpretation give stability to further improvisation without destroying its essential creativeness. Furthermore, there is undoubtedly a carry-over of quality, acquired from the interpretation of the best literature, into the daily speech habits of all sensitive students. To the perfectionist there is from now on no limit to achievement if the stimulus and control of creativeness and technique respectively each contribute to the value of the other.

With interpretational experience comes the best opportunities to formulate theory, not as 'traditional rules' through the application of which a speaker becomes effective, but as the observed bases of dynamic communication. If we are sensible enough to see theory in this way we can claim to be scientific in our methods of improving skills which are essentially human. Similarly with technique.

Techniques should not be regarded as hide-bound habits available to meet particular problems. Technique is the full physical and vocal resourcefulness of an individual to supply fully the demands of a speech situation, restrained only by a sensitive mind which, as the result of wide experience, dictates what, in the circumstances, is fitting.

The acquirement of effective speech is an eclectic pursuit. It does not matter if we draw ideas from physical education, mime, ballet, modern dance, from music or the theatre. It is important that we supplement a kinesthetic approach with other aspects of speech training. (For example, voice productions, and phonemic conventions, may need to be studied from one or other of the authorities available.) What is important is that we work with nature along lines that will lead to the true expression of personality and dynamic communication between personalities, rather than reinforce merely imitated speech patterns. If we clearly understand and apply movement–voice–speech relationships we can realize the benefits of dynamic communication, not least among which are the release of emotional pressure through the safety-valve of adequate speech, the gratification of being able confidently to say what we think, and the glorious awareness of civilized communication with other minds.

Technique re-assessed

Technique seems to have become quite a fearsome notion to many modern artists who tend to see it as the antithesis of creativeness. In the speech arts, especially, technique is today often regarded with mistrust – as a set of suppressive disciplines which will restrict individual expression of personality. As the term itself is bound to have many connotations, perhaps I may be allowed to state what I mean by technique in the context of what I would like to say about its usefulness – even to creative speech.

As I see it, technique derives from theory; it is therefore only as useful as the theory on which it is based is sound. As technique may be assessed only in terms of its contribution to the overall effectiveness of speech, it becomes a confirmation of the validity of the theory which it applies; for as theory tries to explain how speech works, technique offers assistance in turning theory into practice. If our aim is to strengthen the impact of speech, then technique is justified when it increases the effectiveness of speech in communication.

Because of general prejudice, it seems necessary to deal with the main objections – that technique hampers creativeness, destroys individuality and stereotypes interpretation. It seems to me that these objections might be allowed if the acquiring of a set of techniques were intended to become the main prop of unimaginative speakers; for dullards prefer the theoretical, in preference to the creative, attitude. There is this kind of insidious danger in technique, as serious a danger as besets the cartoonist's housewife who, having hit upon one satisfactory way of doing her hair, her cleaning, her cooking and her shopping, is content never, never ever, to try anything new. But this danger springs from an attitude of mind. Let our suburban housewife become aware that her husband and her children are seeking diversion elsewhere as escape from the humdrum routine of her unimaginative ménage and (assuming she is attached to her family, and unless her housekeeping routines have become compulsive) she will, with alacrity, divert her domestic aptitudes into a variety of attractions in an attempt to make her home more attractive than that of the competing 'Jones's' rumpus-room, the youth centre, or the social club. Her attitude, changed by a legitimate motivation, will stimulate the creative exploitation of acquired techniques.

Or to change the illustration in sex, professional status, and technical skill; let us consider the case of a surgeon. Are there not some aspects of surgery which depend upon habitual skills, and others which depend upon the imaginative application of such skills? A patient has the right to expect a surgeon to be dexterous; but he has just as much right to expect a surgeon to be alert to the idiosyncrasies – both physical and psychological – of each individual patient in reaction to any one particular operation. A good surgeon will have acquired manual skills which he will use more or less automatically, so that his concentration may be centred upon the uniqueness of any patient who lies on the operating table before him.

Many other examples could be given, analogous to the complementary relationship between the two essential aspects of technique and creativeness in speech activity. One other example, however, must suffice, and is therefore selected from a profession in which speech plays a dominant part – that of acting. Unless an actor can deal efficiently with such matters as his position on stage, the intelligible articulation of complex consonantal juxtapositions (try that one in passing – just for fun!), and the sustaining of audibility; in fact, until he can manage such things habitually, he stands no chance of creatively interpreting his roles. There was a time in not very distant memory when acting was almost entirely technical, when plays and their presentations were almost completely predictable. Then by a swing of the pendulum, the improvisational approach to acting offered such excitingly dramatic release that technique was blamed for acting which had seemed to be moribund; technical restraint was ignored with the result that actors frequently expressed themselves vigorously without communicating effectively. Dramatic art is now settling into a more sensible equilibrium between the extremes of obsessive technical skill and lively creative imagination. This is not only evidenced by the concern for both aspects in the courses organized by the foremost drama academies, but also by the quality of productions emerging as a result of the recognition of this important duality in the art of acting.

Turning specifically to speech, my experience leads me to argue tenaciously that technique is an essential part of any course in effective speech, and that it should become increasingly significant in a scheme of training which is basically creative. One reason for this has already been suggested in a previous reference to acting. Voice and speech must be habitually sound if they are to function efficiently in an otherwise creative situation. Another reason is that the improvisational approach to speech, with its emphasis on kinesthetically perceived experience, requires us to concentrate on expressing *ourselves* – to our hearts' content. But the purpose of our self-expressing is to strengthen communication, and in communication we must consider *others* as well. The situational differences between studio practice and social communication are very significant. With an old pair of slacks you may be as experimentally creative as you like during improvisational exercises; but it will confuse the processes of communication if you appear in old slacks on the wrong public or social occasions.

If our aim is to be effective in communication (individually contributing with significance in professional situations – whether on stage, at board meetings, on political platforms, in pulpits – whether lecturing, teaching, buying or selling – reading or speaking extemporaneously or from memory our own words or the words of others – cracking jokes or consoling saddened friends – making love or arguing controversially), then in all these situations interest should be evoked through individuality of expression, and communication achieved with the assistance of technique.

The development of technique begins when, during training we learn some skills so well that they become habitual; this is ideal providing we allow the formation only of such habits as will assist, and not replace, creative expression. Generally speaking, technique is concerned with the efficient working of the instruments of expression, keeping them in good order as vehicles of expression ready to offer effective transit for the widest range of communicable thoughts and feelings. Therefore, technique is very much concerned with the body – its control and flexibility; with voice – so that unemoted tone shall be basically pleasant, almost as a musical instrument kept in such good order as to be always ready for the arrival of a musician; with articulation, which should be technically mastered to a degree at which it will never fail to cope with whatever demands may be made of it, even in the most intense utterance. As a pianist (however artistic by temperament) is futile without a piano and without a knowledge of which notes to strike and when, a speaker must either develop to a high degree of precision his combined instruments of body, voice and speech, or he will pay dearly for his neglect. There are problems of two kinds; one arises from the effect of technical domination, the speaker having learned technique as a substitute for creativeness becomes satisfied by making a show of the bare bones of superficial method; the other arises from the technically lazy speaker who, perhaps excitingly creative of mind, fails to communicate because he lacks a responsive instrument through which to release his creativeness intelligibly.

The problem of bridging the gap between the creative workshop and the effective transit of thoughts and feelings in communicational situations is so vital that I am prepared to risk seeming over-prescriptive in summing up the solution to the problem as I have been led to see it:

If you wish to acquire dynamic speech, then from the beginning you must liberate your personality (avoiding all conscious imitation) by creative improvisation of exciting ideas. Through the creative interpretation of good literature, and especially as a result of identification with convincingly portrayed characterizations, the styles of the masters of words will influence your own language habits without conscious effort on your part. Without your realizing it, your speech will become more significant and no less spontaneous.

Keep the habit of improvisation alive; it is of inestimable psychological benefit. Carry it into interpretational reading as a regular habit and, as a result, interpretational ability and extemporaneous speech will mutually benefit. Role-playing in anticipation of formal occasions has helped a great many speakers to realize their own desired image of effectiveness – in law, education, the church, politics, business, or what you will. This does not imply insincerity (it merely increases effectiveness) if a speaker's motives are sound.

Accept only those formal routines which are demanded by the conventions of a speech situation. Such routines need not necessarily be restrictive, whether they have to do with a producer's directions on stage, the regular conduct of public meetings, or any other dictated procedure. It all depends upon your point of view. You can be dynamic by being original within an otherwise dull situation.

Some techniques are indisputably essential. Your voice should be basically pleasant and adequately audible, even when unmotivated. Speech should be habitually intelligible. The tonicity of your body should always be efficiently appropriate.

Perhaps most important of all is the order in which progress is organized. As we exist before becoming conscious of the physiological and psychological systems which make life possible, and well before we began to understand the vital part they play in the business of efficient living, so we should experience the full delight of creative self-expression before we consciously concern ourselves with technical matters – for purposes either of maximum efficiency or of minimum conformity.

Speech education for today

Education in general has great responsibilities in the all-important field of human communications. The day-to-day work of teaching and learning is carried on effectively only if the processes of communication are applied efficiently. The wide diversity of subject-interests and skills among its practitioners calls for co-ordinating communication between them and with those who administer the institutions in which they work. Another kind of communication is necessary if the projected image of education is to evoke the support and encouragement it needs from the public at large. But of utmost importance is the need for education to concern itself, urgently and imaginatively, throughout its range from the infant school to tertiary and adult educational establishments, with the terrible communicational problems of today's world; and it is in attempting to solve them that speech education can offer specific assistance of real worth.

Modern speech education has evolved from a long history of its own during which its aims have sometimes been obscure and frequently confused. In the past, rhetoric, oratory, debating, discussion, declamation, elocution and speech training, have all influenced formal training in speech. In recent years a new spirit has been excitingly noticeable. Speech is seen as creative and individualistic expression of personality; it is acknowledged as the result of psychological processes; it is recognized to be of great sociological significance. Today, a conscientious student of speech education is just as likely to delve into semantics, neuro-muscular physiology, psycho-muscular physiology, psycho-linguistics, and the physics of sound, as his elocutionary predecessors were likely to restrict their studies to a superficial knowledge of breathing, enunciation, the histrionics of recitation, and platform deportment! Above all, responsible speech educationists are whole-heartedly anxious to play their part in solving the communicational problems that beset the world of today, to which end they are prepared to co-operate with similarly concerned colleagues in other areas.

Perhaps the most obviously related field is that of English, the teaching of which has passed through similar changes. The old artificial gulf between the written and the spoken word has been bridged. Oral interpretation of literature is felt to be the most satisfactory means of combining the experiences of writer and reader. Kinesthesis enables a reader to experience empathy without which involvement in described experience is impossible. Nonverbal implications of literature stimulate auditory imagination and cultivate auditory memory, so that nuances of narrative, and especially of dialogue, are effective even during subsequent silent reading. In short, reading becomes active involvement when approached kinesthetically, and literature fulfils one of its most vital functions, that of extending the experience of its readers.

Speech education overlaps physical education. When the former was first attempting to liberate itself from elocution, the latter was beginning to discard 'physical jerks'. Both are now equally convinced that movement is really beneficial only when purposeful, and when imaginatively stimulated.

In art generally and in music particularly there is much coincidence with speech education based on creative improvisation which, if stimulated through one medium, operates in the others. Less tangible notions, such as rhythm in art, may be made real by kinesthetic experience; melodic patterns in music may be more clearly comprehended when conceived as a formalized development of intonation in speech and resulting from the same cause of varying tonicity. Carried to its highest artistic developments in theatre and poetry, speech education offers aesthetic experience arising from kinesthetically aided interpretation of otherwise obscure and evasive symbols.

Speech education therefore may regard itself as being polygamously married to a number of other educational agencies, and should take well into account the desirability of co-operation with its partners. Education will be well served by the correlation of all contributions towards better communications whether from the creative arts, the humanities or the sciences; yet each contribution will be of the nature of its contributor. What then is the particular responsibility of speech training?

Speech education has a very special responsibility in respect of maturation. The whole process of speech education begins by releasing instinctive feelings through kinesic expression, and ends with the mastery of the oral-aural communication of meaningful symbols; it starts by intense self-expression and aims at achieving social skill in adapting to any speech situation likely to be encountered; it covers a range from bluntly utilitarian necessities of day-to-day conversation, to the rarest appreciation of heightened language; it has to do with mental, physical, psychological, sociological and spiritual development; it stimulates acutely perceptive awareness of both sound and meaning; it attempts to balance keen intellect with wholesome emotion; its full study necessitates a wide range of reading in areas such as anthropology, acoustics, poetics, philology, phonetics and neurology. Quite manifestly, speech education is specially involved in the process of maturation which is the general concern of all education.

Communication should also be a general concern of education while being the central purpose of speech education which aims, idealistically, at the mutually helpful interaction of personalities as the result of sincere speaking and sympathetic listening.

The intricately related and all-important ends of individual maturation and profitable communication have frequently been lost sight of in the passing satisfaction of acquiring the many and varied skills by which the ends may be achieved. Many unsound schemes of speech assessment indicate confusion of aims. Any measurement of speech effectiveness should be estimated on the basis of a speaker's ability to communicate. If he communicates persuasively and evocatively, if he arouses empathy in his listeners, then it may be assumed that he has adequately mastered the contributory skills. If he cannot communicate with such manifest success, then an analytical examination of his basic skills should reveal whatever deficiencies are defeating his communicational intentions. Similarly, during maturation (which is a cumulative process of individual development) critical stages may be clearly noticed, but it is the degree of an individual's poise (that desirable balance between defensive, self-effacing apology on the one hand, and over-bearing, arrogant bombast on the other) in a social setting, which is perhaps the most conclusive evidence of satisfactory maturation.

Speech that is adequate assists maturation both intellectually and emotionally, but makes its most needed contribution in the education of the emotions. Education today tends to set greater value on intellectual development than on emotional maturity. It is the interrelated effects of emotional immaturity and deficiency of communication, together with confusion between genuine intellectural prowess and clever sophistication, which has produced a world tragically lacking in human concord. The evidence of disrupted relationships, whether in family, marital, social, industrial, political, national or international affairs is for all to see; and just as obvious is the challenge it presents to those who would claim any responsibility in educating for communication and emotional stability.

Speech education should not be ashamed of its clear title. I regret a current tendency for some of its practitioners to usurp its broad claims under a subject called drama, and I think that the term is semantically ambiguous; it will always be assumed by many to mean the study of plays or the practice of theatre art – and such confusion is dangerous. Dramatic activity as a creative experience has enormous educational potential; it can develop personality readiness for effective speech; but it cannot honestly embrace all that is required for mastery of speech communication. Dramatic activity as an integral part of speech education is one thing, drama as a curriculum subject is another and, if conceived as socio-drama or psycho-drama, then it would be wiser for it to be organized and developed by psychologists than by speech educationists, each of whom may be of great service to the other.

Speech education must insist on clear terms of reference. It needs to be creative, to follow the natural sequence by which experience ultimately is codified into acceptable symbols with minimum loss of spontaneity, to rely upon the stimulus of reactive situations, to vitalize the written word, and to develop sensitivity towards poetry and drama. Above all, speech education should be so organized that always communicational improvement is kept in mind, and maturation fostered.

Speech education has had a tortuous history. For a long time it dabbled with external effects and was too easily satisfied with superficial methods. There is every indication that it is now searching for fundamentals. In my own teaching I am but one of many who have discovered that effective speech is transmuted movement. What I have learned, I have tried to set down in writing. I could have spoken it much better.

Glossary

This glossary is comparatively short. I have omitted most of the terms for which reference may be made to general or special dictionaries, but with two kinds of exception. Some words, germane to my topic (and which I hope have already been clearly explained), have been included for the sake of emphasis. Others, relevant to aspects of speech outside the scope of this book ('enunciation' for instance), have been included where kinesthetic theory also seems to apply.

AESTHETIC EFFECTS of voice and speech arise from such qualities of rhythm, tone, intonation, etc., which appeal pleasantly to a listener's emotions, and which are incidental to meaning and to such feelings as may be derived from meaning.

ARTICULATION. Physiological and organic aspects of the formation of speech sounds which are described in terms of the organs used, and the positions and movements of the organs (cf. Enunciation; Pronunciation).

AUTONOMIC NERVOUS SYSTEM. That part of the nervous system which regulates those aspects of body functions which are not under conscious control; therefore significant in the study of emotion on the basis of external behaviour and bodily changes.

CLIMAX. The arrangement of subject matter in increasing significance, and its establishment as the effect of increasing tonicity on the modulation of tone, rhythm, pitch, etc.

COERCION means: to compel; to enforce. As a coercive speaker is primarily concerned with imposing his will upon others for his own gratification, he is likely to enforce his aims by the use of verbal tricks to by-pass reason, and to superimpose contrived vocal modulation and extraneous gestures for conscious effect. Such speech is not kinesthetically based in that vocal emphasis and kinesic reinforcement are manipulated and do not arise spontaneously from bodily and vocal response to reasonable thought and naturally evoked feeling (cf. Persuasion).

COMMUNICATION. Speech communication basically involves:

A speaker who:
>   encodes ideas into words,
>   speaks words thus organized,
>   reinforcing them paralinguistically according to his convictions, and transmits them through

A channel which is determined by the situations, e.g.:
>   air (in face-to-face conversation), or
>   air and electrical circuitry (as when using a telephone)

A listener who:
>   hears what the speaker has said, decodes the words into received information, interprets their meaning in the light of his own experience, and reacts to the message he has received, thereby supplying

Feed-back to the speaker: which may be stimulating or discouraging, and therefore results in either

Regenerative communication, or

Breakdown of attempted communication.

CONCENTRATION in speech situation results from intense feeling by a speaker for what he is saying, and a strong desire to persuade his listener(s) to concentrate with similar intensity on the content of his utterance. Such concentration is one of the bases of effective communication because it affects the tonicity of both speaker and listener(s) and establishes kinesthetic rapport.

DYNAMIC. In spite of its over-use and frequent mis-use, this term (in its 'force in action' connotation) is relevant to speech which adequately expresses a speaker's mental and emotional power and which, in communication, evokes response from others.

ELOCUTION means 'to speak out', and frequently has been so literally interpreted as to have caused an artificial separation between the controlled modulation of carefully enunciated speech and the psychological processes without which speech becomes pointless. Pre-occupation with elocution thus leads to affectation by ignoring the processes by which speech is integrated within the personality of the speaker.

EMPATHY is the result of our kinesthetic sensations evoked by the overt behaviour of others enabling us to 'feel' ourselves into their feelings and leading to our identifying ourselves with them in what they are experiencing.

EMPHASIS. The organizing of significance relative to the comparative importance of words as spoken. The variations of voice and speech by which emphasis is established arise from causal changes in muscular tonicity which reflect the fluctuations of intensity experienced by a speaker or reader who is genuinely involved in what he is saying or reading.

ENUNCIATION is concerned with the efficiency with which intended phonemes are uttered (cf. Articulation; Pronunciation). Intelligibility of utterance is dependent upon the tonicity of the moveable organs responsible for articulation (tongue, lips, soft palate and lower jaw). Hypotonicity will reduce intelligibility; hypertonicity will impede fluency and destroy rhythm in speech. Directly, enunciation requires a 'tonicity norm' with a range which can cope with 'tense' and 'lax' vowels (e.g. as in *neat* and *knit* respectively) as well as with the relative muscular pressures of consonants.

EXTEMPORANEOUS describes a style of speaking which aims at apparent spontaneity. It applies to interpretational speech because spontaneous speech is naturally extemporaneous; whereas prepared speaking is usually (with exceptions such as a 'formal address' or a learned paper') more convincing if it seems to be spontaneous. Some professional speakers, notably from among actors, claim that if excellent techniques are perfectly timed (i.e. if the co-ordination of movement and speech is consciously organized as if it were taking place in real life), then an impression of spontaneity results. This external approach fools some of the people some of the time. Interpretational speech which has become habitually kinesthetic will always have extemporaneous flexibility, and will in fact be (rather than seem to be) spontaneous, as it requires a speaker to be involved with the intellectual meaning and emotional reactions of words as well as with their linguistic and paralinguistic expression – proper timing being automatic and not merely calculated (cf. Spontaneity).

GESTURE. Expressive changes in the muscular set of the body, in excess of those which are transmuted into modulation of voice and speech, are to be observed as a kinesic accompaniment of the spoken word; these, and also overt bodily changes which mimetically substitute for speech, are generally referred to as gestures. (Facial expression literally is 'facial gesture', but is not usually referred to as such.)

HYPERTONICITY. Muscular tension in excess of that required for immediate purposes.

HYPOTONICITY. Muscular tension insufficient for that required for immediate purposes.

IMPROVISATION. Exploration of ideas and feelings through dramatic experimentation. Improvisation stimulates imagination and, when used impressionistically, its creative benefits are enormous. When improvisation is developed into a set piece, it becomes a creative approach to interpretation.

INFLECTION. A change of pitch, during the speaking of a word or syllable of a word, due to the fluctuating tonicity of a speaker affecting the tension applied to his vocal cords by the muscles of his larynx.

INTERPRETATION. The reading or speaking of words scripted previous to their utterance. (As different from the spontaneous expression of thought and feeling organized more or less concurrently with the experience evoking it.)

INTONATION. The overall 'melodic' effect of pitch change in connected speech; it embraces inflection and indicates relative significances by a tendency for pitch to rise and fall consistently with emphasis, resulting from increased and decreased tonicity of a speaker to 'make his points' and not to distract from them by sustaining undue interest on subsidiary words.

KINESIOLOGY. Science of motion. Human kinesiology

is basic to the understanding of the skilful and efficient use of the body as an expressive agent.

KINESIS. Indication of muscular state or change of state by body set or movement; e.g. stance, posture, gesture, facial expression.

KINESTHETIC FEED-BACK. Control of movement by its correction, as the result of kinesthetic information of activity, to what is intended. Apart from its kinesic importance, pronunciation, articulation and enunciation are largely controlled by kinesthetic feed-back to conform to what is acoustically monitored.

KINESTHETIC PERCEPTION. Awareness of muscular activity as the result of changes of tension stimulating kinesthetic sensory structures incorporated within muscles.

MATURATION. The process towards, or the attainment of, the state of complete personal development. As the gratification of needs (such as a sense of 'belonging', the esteem of others, self-respect, and aesthetic experience) is essential to maturation, the importance of speech in the process can hardly be over-stressed. Adequate speech ability is indispensable to the gratification of many needs.

MODULATION. The transfer of fluctuating bodily intensity to voice and speech to indicate the relative significances of words in terms of their meaning and of the speaker's emotional reaction to them.

PARALINGUISTIC: describes the effect of muscular tension merging into voice and speech and therefore adding significance to the spoken word by kinesthetically stimulated modulation.

PERSUASION. Literally, to persuade is to induce someone by argument into doing something; to convince; to influence his mind. Unlike coercion, persuasion through speech implies worthy motives (on the part of the speaker) and clear thinking (of both speaker and listener). It involves tolerance and permissiveness. A speaker assumes that his statement will not be accepted until his listeners are convinced of its worth by their own efforts of discrimination. The listener is, as it were, induced to consider; not cajoled into accepting without consideration. To be persuasive, a speaker needs to be sincere and, because sincerity is the consistency of overt expression with inner thoughts and feelings, kinesthetic method is likely to lead to reasonable persuasiveness – because it aims at the natural linking of inner experience with the overt expression of it (cf. Coercion).

PHONEME. A class of speech sounds usually heard as the same, even though acoustically varied as the result of context, e.g. 'b' as in bad, bid, bend, cub.

PRONUNCIATION. The pattern of a speaker's phonemes, stresses and inflections in relation to an accepted standard. Conscious adjustment to a pronunciation pattern is effected by a combined process of aural monitoring and kinesthetic feed-back (cf. Articulation; Enunciation).

RELAXATION. Diminution of tonicity.

RHYTHM is a basically regular movement modified by emotion. In speech, such movement patterns are transferred to utterance and are heard as vocal changes on a time base. Word choice and order may either encourage or obstruct rhythm, but words may be patterned not only to make sense, but also to reveal the emotions of the speaker. In impressive prose, sentences form rhythmical units. In poetry there is generally an extended overall patterning. Possibly the greatest damage to speech rhythm is done when verse is analysed according to its basic metrical pattern. It is important that rhythm be conceived as an instinctive expression of emotion to be perceived through kinesthesis.

SPEECH THERAPY. The highly specialized treatment of speech defects; functional (as when a normal organ of speech is linguistically ineffective), organic (as when an organ of speech is malformed or atrophied), or psychogenetic (of mental origin or due to nervous disorder). Kinesthesis is significant in many therapeutic treatments.

SPONTANEITY: a characteristic of speech which is evoked by a situation in which utterance is more or less immediate. Apart from emotional exclamations and day-to-day social clichês, absolute spontaneity is theoretically impossible, because inter-related organization of thoughts and words always takes place before utterance. The term is frequently used to differentiate speech which is organized in the situation which evokes it, from speech which is prepared in anticipation of a situational requirement (cf. Extemporaneous).

TONICITY. The degree of muscular tonus sufficient for effort and which is neither inadequate (resulting in ineffectuality) nor excessive (causing waste of energy, or impedance of movement due to rigidity). An efficient state of readiness for movement response to stimulus (cf. Hypertonicity; Hypotonicity).

TONUS. The condition, due to stimuli from the nervous system, which keeps muscles in a state of readiness for action.

Short Reading List

STUDY IN COLLATORAL AREAS IS ESSENTIAL IF experience of speech and the understanding of its processes are to be meaningful. The following titles are representative of books dealing appropriately with communication theory, physiology, semantics, movement, voice and speech technique, and with the teaching of oral English.

DAVID K. BERLO *The Process of Communication* Holt, Rinehart & Winston

ROSE BRUFORD *Teaching Mime* Methuen

GRETA COLSON *Speech Practice* Museum Press

JOHN C. CONDON, JUN. *Semantics and Communication* Collier–Macmillan

S. I. HAYAKAWA *Language in Thought and Action* Allen & Unwin

JOHN HODGSON and ERNEST RICHARDS *Improvisation* Methuen

DAVID HOLBROOK *English for Maturity* Cambridge University Press

A. MUSGRAVE HORNER *Speech Training* A. & C. Black

RUDOLF LABAN *Modern Educational Dance* Macdonald & Evans

OTTO LOWENSTEIN *The Senses* Penguin

S. S. STEVENS *Handbook of Experimental Psychology* Wiley

Index

Acting, 111, 117, 118
Aesthetics of voice and speech, 129
Afterwards (Excerpt), Thomas Hardy, 69
Ancient Greek culture, 12
Articulation, 129
    Effect of tonicity on, 13
Atmosphere
    Movement as basis of, 20
Autonomic nervous system, 28, 129

Bells of Heaven, The, Ralph Hodgson, 70–71
Boots (Excerpt), Rudyard Kipling, 65
Breath control, 29
Bronowski, J. (quoted), 40
Brumana (Excerpt), James Elroy Flecker, 60
Builders, The (Excerpt), Laurence Binyon, 68

Chrysalids, The (Excerpt), John Wyndham, 82
Class-room restrictions, 15
Climax, 50, 103, 130
Coercion, 9, 10, 31, 130

Coal (Excerpt), John Gould Fletcher, 67–8
Communication, 10, 130, 131
    Kinesthetic, 14, 18–21, 40
Concentration, 131
Creative experience, 23
    Basis of interpretation, 60–94

Discovery, The, J. C. Squire, 71–2
Drama, 36, 87–94
    Creative interpretation of, 87–94
Driving Sheep, Rose Macaulay, 73–4
Dynamic speech, 31, 36, 115, 131
    arises from kinesthesis, 38
    principles of, 109–15

Elocution, 131
    danger of, 14
Emotion,
    basis of paralinguistic reinforcement, 34, 36
    emotion memory 53
    intensity, 40
    William James quoted, 110–11

Empathy, 131

Emphasis, 103, 131

English language and literature, 123

Enunciation, 132

Environment,
    effect of, 10–11
    for improvisation, 44

Expression through movement, releases expression through speech, 12

Extemporaneous speech, 132

Facial expression,
    effect on tone, 13

Fallen Cities, Gerald Gould, 75

Flannan Isle (Excerpt), W. W. Gibson, 60

Gesture, 132–3
    assists fluency, 19–20
    basis of speech, 12
    timing of, 13
    facilitates vocal stress, 20
    Paget's 'Oral Gesture' theory, 21
    substitute for speech, 20
    Wundt's 'Gesture' theory, 21

Happiness, A. A. Milne, 64

Henry V (Excerpt), William Shakespeare, 90–91

Hero Entombed (Excerpt), Peter Quennell, 61

Homage to the British Museum (Excerpt), William Epson, 61

Hound of Heaven, The (Excerpt), Francis Thompson, 61

Hypertonicity, 47, 113, 133

Identification, 11

Imitation,
    conscious, 11
    unconscious, 10, 11

Improvisation, 43–59, 97–9, 113, 133

Inflection, 29, 34, 38, 105, 133

Intensity, 103

Internalized movement, 81

Interpretation, 60, 133
    creative interpretation, 60
    of drama, 36, 87–94
    of poetry, 36, 60–81
    of prose, 81–7
    as vicarious experience, 76

Intonation, 38, 105, 133

Involvement, 11
    through kinesthesis, 19, 38

Isometric contraction, 45

James, William (quoted), 110–11

Keats, John, 76–7

Kinesiology, 133–4

Kinesis, 134

Kinesthesis,
    basis of communication, 31, 40
    link between impression and expression, 28, 31, 33–41

Kinesthetic feed-back, 30, 134

Kinesthetic perception, 134

Kinesthetic rapport, 14, 19, 41, 52

King Lear (Excerpt), William Shakespeare, 88

Laboratory, The (Excerpt), Robert Browning, 70

Linguistic sequence, 34

Lorna Doone (Excerpt), R. D. Blackmore, 83
Lotus Eaters, The (Excerpt), Alfred Tennyson, 61
Lyrical poetry, 74–5, 81

Macbeth (Excerpt), William Shakespeare, 93
Maturation, 11, 110, 124, 134
Maud (Excerpt), Alfred Tennyson, 69–70
Measurement of speech effectiveness, 101, 106–8
Modulation, 134
    kinesthetically based, 29–30, 102–5
    result of emotion and tonicity, 37
Mood,
    movement as basis of, 20
Movement, voice and speech relationships, 12, 13, 15, 17, 19, 22, 113, 115
Motivation,
    of improvisation, 48–59
Murder in the Cathedral (Excerpt), T. S. Eliot, 89
Music of Sundry Kinds (Excerpt), Thomas Ford, 70

Ode to a Nightingale, John Keats, 77–80
Old Woman of the Roads, The (Excerpt), Padraic Colum, 60
Origins of language, 12
Our Mutual Friend (Excerpt), Charles Dickens, 83–4

Pace, 39, 103–4
Paget, Sir Richard,
    'Oral gesture' theory, 21

Paralinguistic effects, 34–41, 134
Pause, 37–8, 105
Persuasion, 10, 31, 134–5
Pharynx,
    fundamental resonator, 39
    response to emotion, 39
Phoneme, 135
Phrasing, 104–5
    kinesthetically based, 37
Pilgrim's Progress, The (Excerpt), John Bunyan, 86–7
Pitch, 38, 39–40, 105
Poetry, 61–2
    creative interpretation of, 36, 60–81
Poison Tree, A (Excerpt), William Blake, 70
Pronunciation, 135
Propaganda, 9
Prose,
    creative interpretation of, 81–7
Public solitude, 51

Rapport, 14, 19, 41
Relaxation, 42–6, 113, 135
Return, The (Excerpt), Arthur Symons, 61
Rhythm, 30, 62–7, 104, 135–6
Role playing, 99, 120
Romeo and Juliet (Excerpt), William Shakespeare, 91–2

Saint Joan (Excerpt), Bernard Shaw, 88–9
Semantics, 27
Senses,
    sensory perception, 18
    sensory imagery, 18, 111
    sense organs, 33
    alerting the senses, 52–5

Senses—*contd.*
    sense deprivation, 89
    sense unit; *see* – phrasing
Sincerity, 10, 33
Soliloquy, 92–3
Song of the Shirt, The (cited),
    Thomas Hood, 66–7
Speech,
    assessment, 101, 106–8, 125
    education, 10, 121–7
    everyday speech, 95–109
    freedom of, 10
    motivated, 27
    unmotivated, 25
Speech therapy, 12, 136
Speech training,
    danger if superficial, 11
    essential for most speakers,
    11, 56
Spontaneity, 136
Stanislawsky, Constantin
    (quoted), 53
Stress, 30, 34, 38, 103

Teaching,
    empirical, 17
    responsible, 26
    speech from movement, 112

Technique, 114–21
Technology,
    effect on style of speech, 16,
    20–21
Tess of the D'Ubrervilles (Excerpt),
    Thomas Hardy, 85–6
Theory, 24–31
Tone colour, 30, 39, 102
Tonicity, 136
    effect on vocal tone, 18, 30
    effect on enunciation, 30
    effect on stress, 30
    tonus consciousness, 45–7,
    52
    individual tonicity norm,
    113
Tyger, The (cited), William
    Blake, 65–6

Vocal tone, 13, 38, 39, 102

*Where We Are Right and Where
    We Are Wrong* (Excerpt),
    Arthur Guiterman, 70
Wooden Horse, The (Excerpt),
    Eric Williams, 84
Wundt, William (quoted), 21